RICHMOND
ESSENTIAL
English

Pssst! If you start your English course late or finish it early, ask your teacher for a copy of the keys. Then you can complete Essential English 2 and check all your answers yourself.

GREAT! WHAT ABOUT YOU YES, OF COURSE
SEE YOU LATER I LOVE IT THAT'S A GREAT IDEA
HAVE A GOOD TIME! HAVE A GOOD HOLIDAY
HERE YOU ARE HAVE A GOOD HOLIDAY I LOVE IT LET'S GO
OH, YOU'RE RIGHT IT'S THE SAME IN MY LANGUAGE OH, REALLY?
HURRY UP! HAVE A GOOD HOLIDAY OH, REALLY? LET'S GO
EXCUSE ME, PLEASE! OH

ELEMENTARY
Coursebook with CD-ROM

COURSE

2

Main author: **PAUL SELIGSON**

Richmond
PUBLISHING

www.richmondelt.com/essentialenglish

Course book contents map

3

An excellent place to learn English

Reading

1 What can you see in the photos? Think of five adjectives to describe them. What do you know about Malta?

2 Read the webpage quickly. Cover the text and, in pairs, remember all you can.

Malta English School (MES)

(1) The beautiful island of Malta sits in (2) the middle of (3) the Mediterranean between Sicily and Libya. It's (4) a bilingual country and is a member of (5) the EU.

It's (6) an excellent place to learn English – or Maltese! With wonderful beaches, lovely weather, great food, friendly people, (7) a fabulous history and fantastic nightlife, it's easy to understand why thousands of international visitors come to Malta every year to study English. And they often come back again and again, too!

3 (1.1) Listen and check. Are all your ideas from Exercise 1 in the text? Would you like to study in Malta? Why / Why not?

Listening

4 (1.2) Listen to part of an interview with a student at MES. Circle the correct options.

1 What does Ewa like doing in her free time?

water-skiing   skiing   surfing   windsurfing

2 Why does she want to learn English?

*for work   to study in English   to translate
to travel   to meet people*

3 Why's she studying in Malta?

the weather   the food   the people   the cost

> **Tip**
>
> *to* + verb   I'm here **to learn** English.
>
> *for* + noun   I study English **for** my job.

5 Listen again. Write the questions you hear. In pairs, ask and answer.

What nationality are you?

6 Tell the class three interesting things about your partner.

Olga wants to learn English to understand films and songs and because she likes learning languages. She speaks Russian, Turkish and a little French, too.

Grammar

7 Underline 10 adjectives in the text in Exercise 2. What noun does each adjective refer to?

Beautiful refers to the island of Malta.

> **Articles**
>
> Use **a** / **an** for singular nouns when we don't know which:
>
> Amy works in **a** bank.
>
> Use **the** for singular and plural nouns when we know which:
>
> Amy works in **the** bank near my house.
>
> Don't use articles
> 1 when we talk generally: I hate banks.
> 2 with names: I bank with HSBC.

AB, p. 79. Ex. 4 ▶

8 Read the Grammar box. Study the text in Exercise 2 again. In pairs, answer the questions.

1 Why do we use the articles numbered 1–7?

We use 'the' because we know which island. It's the only island with the name Malta.

2 Why don't we use an article with these nouns in the text?

> Malta   Sicily   Libya   English   beaches
> food   nightlife   visitors

We don't use an article for 'Malta' because it's a name.

> **Tip**
>
> Pronounce *the* as /ðiː/ before a vowel sound.
>
> the EU   the internet   the only island

Speaking

9 (1.3)–(1.5) What colour's your country's flag? Word Bank 1, p. 64.

10 In groups, find out about each other. Give your opinions about:

> interesting people   islands   countries
> beaches   nightlife   food   films

A: *My grandmother's alive. She's 97 and she's very strong!*

B: *Wow! That's wonderful! Does she live alone?*

1B What are you doing?

Reading

1 Do you know these songs? What's your favourite song at the moment? What do you think is the world's favourite song?

Imagine   *Smells like Teen Spirit*   *Satisfaction*

2 Read the text to check your answer. Does any information there surprise you?

3 In groups, ask and answer. Any coincidences?

   1 When's your birthday? Do you know anybody with the same birthday as you?

   2 Do you usually enjoy your birthday? What do you usually do?

   3 Does somebody usually sing 'Happy Birthday' to you?

Listening

4 Match the verb phrases and the pictures, A–F.

   _E_ wait for a bus   ___ sit in a traffic jam

   ___ run on a machine   ___ have a shower

   ___ wake up   ___ talk to somebody on the phone

5 (1.6) Listen to Jane talking to her friends and number the pictures B–F, in order 1–5. What do you think of Jane's friends?

Q **What is the world's favourite song?**

A More people sing 'Happy Birthday to You' than any other song – there are versions in many different languages. And the number-one day to sing it is … 5th October. That's because it's the most common birthday, at least in the USA. Why? Who knows? Perhaps it's because it's about nine months after the New Year holiday!? And, apart from February 29th, the least common birthday in the USA is May 22nd. But we have no idea why – do you?

Grammar

6 (1.7) Listen and complete Jane's words. Who's she talking to?

   1 _'_ w _ _ _ _ _ _ _ for you! What _ _ _ you _ _ _ _ _ _ at the gym?
     A _ _ you _ _ _ _ _ _?

   2 I can't believe it! Y _ _'_ _ sl _ _ _ _ _ _ _!

7 Read the Grammar box and circle the correct options.

Present continuous	
What **are** you do**ing**?	I'm watch**ing** TV now.
Are you enjoy**ing** this exercise?	Yes, I **am**. / No, I'm **not**.
I'm **not** study**ing** at the moment.	

* Use the Present continuous to talk about actions which **are / aren't** in progress.
* Use *have / be* in the present **+ verb + –ing** / **+ verb.**

   (AB, p. 80. Ex. 2 ▶)

8 Look at the six pictures opposite for 20 seconds. Cover them. In pairs, ask and answer.

   A: *What's Ben doing? / What are Kim and Sam doing?*

   B: *He's … . / They're … .*

9 (1.8)–(1.9) Listen. Where are these four people? What are they doing? Word Bank 2, p. 65.

   1 He's on a _____ . He's _____ .

Speaking

10 In pairs, compare what your friends and family are / aren't probably doing now. Any coincidences?

A: *My sister's at work, but I'm sure she isn't working. She's probably checking her e-mails.*

B: *Really. What does she do?*

A: *She's a hotel receptionist. What about your brothers and sisters? Are they working?*

11 Tell the class two interesting things you now know about your partner.

A: *It's Theo's birthday tomorrow. His mother's retired. She loves cooking and he thinks she's probably making a birthday cake now!*

1C Money: save a lot, spend a little

Reading

1 (1.10) How many plastic cards do you have with you today? Word Bank 3, p. 66.

2 (1.11) Listen and read. Complete the chart with words from the text.

This week, we look at the USA and ask: 'What do Americans spend their money on?'

Today, a typical American family spends 12.8% of their money on food, 5.7% on health care and 5.7% on clothes. They spend a lot on housing and transport: 32.7% and 18.0%, but surprisingly they spend very little on education, only 2.0%, and only 5.1% on entertainment.

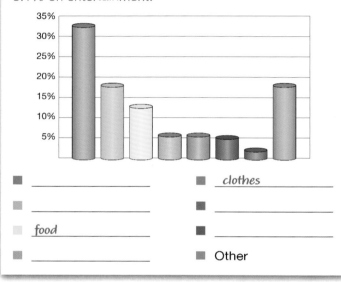

■ _____   ■ _clothes_

■ _____   ■ _____

■ _food_   ■ _____

■ _____   ■ Other

Tip
% = per cent
1.6 = one point six

Speaking

3 What do you spend your money on? Calculate your percentages. In pairs, compare answers.

A: *How much do you spend on food?*

B: *I spend about 20% of my money on food. And you?*

A: *I don't. I spend … .*

4 Tick (✓) the sentences you think are good advice. In pairs, compare answers. Try to say why.

Good or bad advice?

1 ☐ Spend money on essential things only.

2 ☐ Always pay by credit card. Never pay cash.

3 ☐ Don't give children a lot of pocket money.

4 ☐ Always pay your bills on time.

5 ☐ Borrow money from a friend when you're broke.

6 ☐ Try to save 10% of your salary every month.

7 ☐ Don't ask for a discount in shops and markets.

A: *I think number one is good advice.*

B: *Yes, I agree if you don't have a lot of money. / No, I don't agree.*

A: *Why not?*

B: *Because we sometimes need to have fun!*

Tip
The imperative has only one positive and one negative form. Is your language the same?

+ Ask the teacher.
– Don't ask the teacher.

8

Listening

5 (1.12) Listen to Max, Jo and Sara. Write T (true) or F (false). Explain why.

1 Max doesn't have any free time. ____

2 Max spends a lot of money on entertainment. ____

3 Jo doesn't give her children any pocket money. ____

4 Jo often borrows some money from friends. ____

5 Sara needs some money. ____

6 Sara always asks for a discount. ____

Grammar

6 In pairs, complete the Grammar box with *Max*, *Jo* or *Sara*. Listen again and check.

a lot of, some, any		
✓✓✓✓	_____ has **a lot of** bills.	
✓✓✓✓	_____ needs **a lot of** time.	
✓✓✓✓	_____ gives her children **some** pocket money. _____ has **some** savings.	
✗	_____ doesn't want **any** problems. _____ doesn't have **any** credit cards.	

AB, p. 81. Ex. 4 ▶

Pronunciation

7 (1.13) Are the pink words in the Grammar box stressed? What sound do they have in common? Listen and repeat the first four sentences.

Speaking

8 In groups, compare what you have / don't have at home. Use these nouns. How much do you spend on the things in column 2?

1	2
bills	books
boxes	CDs, DVDs and computer games
cash	clothes
papers	food
pictures	furniture
photos	magazines and newspapers
space	music

A: *I don't have a lot of bills now because I'm living with my parents. And you?*

B: *I have some bills, but I'm OK. I don't have a lot of books at home.*

C: *I have a lot of boxes of old papers and magazines! A lot!*

A: *How much do you spend on DVDs?*

B: *Not a lot.*

C: *Really? I don't buy any DVDs ... .*

Can I try them on?

Speaking

1 (1.14) What are you wearing? Word Bank 4, p. 67.

2 In pairs, ask and answer. Remember one unusual thing to tell the class.

> ### Are you into clothes?
>
> **1** What's your favourite clothes shop? What do you usually buy there?
> **2** Do you like T-shirts? When do you wear them?
> **3** How many pairs of shoes do you have?
> **4** How often do you wear a suit, a skirt or a dress? How about jeans?
> **5** What colour clothes do / don't you like wearing?

Listening

3 (1.15) Listen to Ben buying some new clothes for a holiday.

1 Which two items does he want to look at?
2 How much are they?

4 Read and circle the correct option. Listen again, check and repeat.

Assistant: Can I help you?

Ben: (¹)*This / These* is a really nice T-shirt. How much (²)*is it / are they*?

Assistant: Which (³)*one / ones*?

Ben: The white (⁴)*one / ones*.

Assistant: (⁵)*It's / They're* £21.99.

Ben: Cool! I'll take (⁶)*it / them*.

Assistant: Anything else?

Ben: Yes! I really like (⁷)*these / those* trainers (⁸)*here / over* there. How much (⁹)*is / are* the black (¹⁰)*one/ ones*?

Assistant: (¹¹)*It's / They're* only £32.49 at the moment.

Ben: (¹²)*That's / They're* great. They're really cheap!

Assistant: Would you like to try (¹³)*it / them* on?

Ben: Yes, please.

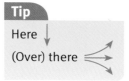

Tip

Here ↓

(Over) there ⇒

Grammar

5 Complete the Grammar box with words from Exercise 4.

Singular	Plural
a T-shirt	T-shirts
this	_____
_____	those
it	_____
them	them
it's	_____
_____ _____	they aren't
_____ _____ ...?	Are they ...?
	_____
one	
Which _____?	_____ _____

✓ I like the white **one(s)**.

✗ ~~I like the white(s).~~

(AB, p. 82. Ex. 3 ▶)

Speaking

6 How much is it? In pairs, ask and answer about the items in Exercise 3.

A: *How much is / are the ...?*

B: *Which one / ones?*

A: *The white one / ones.*

B: *It's / They're £27.99.*

7 ▢ Get a card from your teacher. Imagine you are shopping.
A: You're the shop assistant. Help the customer.
B: You're the customer. Buy the clothes you need. When you finish, swap roles.

A: *Can I help you?*

B: *Yes, how much ...?*

1e

There are hundreds of restaurants

Reading

1 (1.16) Name a building or place beginning with the letters *b*, *c*, *h*, *l* and *s*. Word Bank 5, p. 68.

2 In pairs, ask and answer about London.

   1 What do you know about the city?

   2 Would you like to go there? Why / Why not?

   3 What can you see in the photos?

3 (1.17) Listen and read about London. Write T (true) or F (false).

   1 There are two Information Centres in London. ____

   2 It's a good idea to buy theatre tickets in advance. ____

   3 Covent Garden is a restaurant. ____

   4 You can find all types of food and drinks. ____

   5 *Travel Card* is another name for the London underground. ____

London – one of the world's great cities

Five tips for you to enjoy this wonderful city

- **Sightseeing**. London is full of famous sights: Big Ben, Tower Bridge, The London Eye, St Paul's Cathedral … and there are over 200 museums! Get a bus tour to see them all. If you need help, there are many Information Centres in the city. Look for this sign 𝒊.

- **Theatres & nightlife**. In London's West End alone, there are about 50 theatres and a lot of pubs and nightclubs. The theatres have fantastic shows. There's only one problem: it's often difficult to get tickets. Buy in advance!

- **Shopping**. Shops? Everywhere! In Oxford Street, King's Road, Covent Garden, South Kensington … and of course there's Harrods. And there are lots of lovely street markets, too, especially in Camden and Notting Hill.

- **Eating & drinking**. Hungry? No problem! There are hundreds of excellent restaurants everywhere! From Chinese to Italian, sandwiches, curry and fish and chips to the fabulous, Michelin three-star Restaurant Gordon Ramsay in Chelsea. Don't forget pubs have good, cheap food, too. But remember, the beer isn't always cold!

- **Getting around**. It's best to use buses or the underground. People in London call it 'the Tube'. Look for this sign ⊖. But transport is expensive, so buy a travel card at any station.

Look at www.londontown.com for more information.

4 Read the text again. Find:

- two words to complete the compass
- two phrases meaning *many*
- two tips you think are very useful.

Pronunciation

5 (1.18) Listen and repeat. Are the vowel sounds in each pair the same (S) or different (D)?

1 sight / sign ☐
2 buy / eye ☐
3 lovely / hungry ☐
4 full / bus ☐
5 pub / food ☐
6 tour / tower ☐
7 beer / theatre ☐

Grammar

6 (1.19) Read the Grammar box. Underline five more examples in the text in Exercise 3. Listen, check and repeat.

> **there is / there are**
>
> Singular: **There's** only one problem.
> Plural: **There are** over 200 museums.
>
> **Contractions**
> there's = there is
>
> ✓ **There are** lovely markets.
> ✗ Have / It is / There is lovely markets.

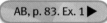 AB, p. 83. Ex. 1 ▶

Speaking

7 In groups, tell each other about places you know around the world. Use *There's / There are.*

1 a great museum
2 lots of modern buildings
3 a fabulous art gallery
4 wonderful markets
5 a lovely old building

There's a great museum in New Orleans. It's a jazz museum.

Grammar

8 (1.20) Match the pictures and the sentences, 1–4. Listen and check.

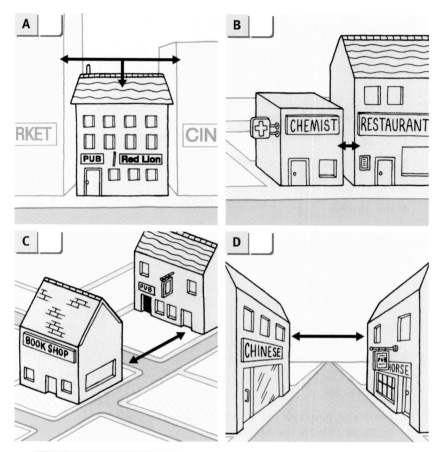

> **Prepositions of place**
>
> 1 There's a pub op**posite** the Chinese restaurant.
> 2 There's another restaurant **next to** the chemist's.
> 3 There's a bookshop **near** the pub.
> 4 There's another pub be**tween** the supermarket and the cinema.

AB, p. 83. Ex. 4 ▶

9 Test a partner. Ask *Who* or *What* + prepositions.

A: *What's opposite the door?*
B: *The window. Who's next to me and near the teacher?*

10 🗋 Get a card from your teacher. In pairs, ask and answer.

11 In groups, talk about your hometown or area. Think of five tips to put in a blog for tourists.

A: *There are great Turkish restaurants in the city centre. They open late and have good, cheap food.*
B: *There's a club, Sax 'n' Tracks, near my flat. It has cheap drinks and great music. Go before 11 p.m. and it's free.*

Have you got a map?

Listening

1 In pairs, ask and answer.

  1 How often do you get a taxi?

  2 What do / don't you like about taxis and taxi drivers in your country?

2 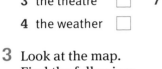 **1.21** Listen to a tourist and a taxi driver. Tick (✓) what they talk about.

  1 a map ☐   **5** shopping ☐

  2 her daughter ☐   **6** a restaurant ☐

  3 the theatre ☐   **7** money ☐

  4 the weather ☐

3 Look at the map. Find the following:

  1 an underground station

  2 an Information Centre

  3 a bank

4 **1.22** Listen again to the dialogue in Exercise 2. Circle the correct option. Word Bank 6A, p. 69.

  1 There's an underground station *opposite / next to* the hotel.

  2 There's an Information Centre *in front of / behind* the hotel.

  3 There's a bank *outside / next to* the Information Centre.

  4 The Information Centre is *near / between* the bank and the café.

  5 Her daughter lives *under / near* the river.

  6 There's a doorman *inside / outside* the hotel.

Grammar

5 Complete the Grammar box with *is*, *are*, *aren't*, *a*, *any* and *there*.

Questions and short answers					
singular	❷	___ there	__ café __ bank	around here? near here?	Yes, there ___ . No, there ___ .
plural		___ there	_____ good hotels _____ museums	in this area?	Yes, there ___ . No, there ___ .

1.23 Listen and check. Link *there* with the vowel sounds after it in questions and answers.

6 Think about the facilities near your home and make two lists.

Three good things you can find there	Three good things you can't find there

In pairs, ask and answer. Are the facilities near your homes similar?

A: *Is there a good restaurant near your flat?*

B: *Yes, there is. There's one in the next street, but it's very expensive. / No, there isn't.*

7 Listen again to the dialogue in Exercise 2. Write T (true) or F (false).

1 The tourist has got six days' holiday. ____

2 She hasn't got any friends or family in London. ____

3 She hasn't got a good map. ____

4 She has got the exact money for the taxi. ____

8 Complete the Grammar box with *hasn't*, *have*, *'s*, *'ve*, *has*, *a* and *any*.

have got	
➕	I / You / We / They _____ got __ map. He / She / It _____ got children.
➖	I / You / We / They _____ got __ ticket. He / She / It _____ got ____ money.
❓	_____ you got __ bag?
✅	Yes, I / we have.
❌	No, I / we _____ .
❓	_____ he got __ computer?
✅❌	Yes, he _____ . No, he hasn't.

Contractions
's got = ___ got   've got = ____ got

9 Which rule's correct? Find examples from the dialogue in the audioscript (1.21) on page 107.

1 Use *have got* or *have* to talk about possessions.

2 Use *have got* or *have* to talk about regular actions.

10 Tick (✓) the correct sentences. Correct the wrong ones.

1 I've got two dogs. ☐

2 She's got a shower every morning. ☐

3 They haven't got breakfast at 7.30. ☐

4 You've got a nice flat. ☐

11 Read the Tip box and then do activities 1–3.

> **Tip**
>
> Some nouns have a plural with *s* (map / maps) and some don't have a plural (water). We call these 'countable' or 'uncountable' nouns.

1 Put the words in the box into the correct lists.

> diary   toothbrush   newspaper   water   tissues
> money   soap   dictionary   change   shampoo

countable	**uncountable**

2 Add three more words of your own to each list.

3 Ask your partner about the words on the lists.

A: *Have you got a newspaper with you today?*

B: *Yes, I have. What about you?*

Speaking

12 You're flying to London for a four-day / three-night holiday. Apart from clothes, list eight things to take with you.
In pairs, ask what's on your partner's list. How many of your things are the same?

A: *Have you got a guidebook?*

B: *No, I haven't. I can google for information when I arrive. Have you got any ...?*

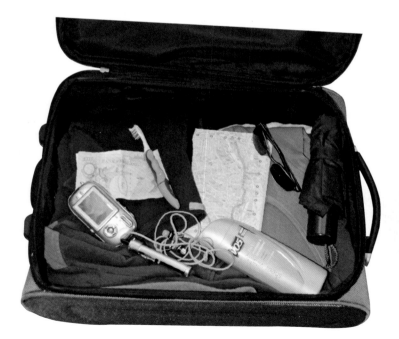

Revision

1A 1 Choose the correct words to complete the sentences. In pairs, compare answers.

1 Lee's really _____. He reads a lot and he always knows the answers to our teacher's questions.

  a intelligent   **b** strong   **c** fast

2 Come to the concert with me! The tickets are _____ .

  a easy   **b** cheap   **c** weak

3 Jan's always _____ for class. I think she goes to lots of parties!

  a late   **b** slow   **c** short

4 Dan's quite _____ because his girlfriend is in the USA with her parents.

  a bad   **b** late   **c** sad

5 Petra loves her boyfriend's _____ eyes.

  a purple   **b** orange   **c** blue

2 In pairs, ask and answer. After five questions, swap roles.

A: Close your eyes.

B: Ask the colours of things in the room.

A: *What colour's the teacher's bag?*

B: *It's brown.*

A: *What colours are my pens?*

3 Complete the text with *a / the* or *0* (no article). In pairs, compare answers.

In summer, we usually go to (1) _____ Spain for our holiday. We go to (2) _____ lovely town near (3) _____ mountains. We stay at (4) _____ hotel just outside (5) _____ town. It has (6) _____ amazing food. Tom and I go for lots of walks, and our children often go swimming in (7) _____ river near (8) _____ hotel. I don't go swimming because (9) _____ river is very cold!

1B 4 🗌 Play MAKE A PHRASE in teams. Get a card from your teacher. In teams, make three phrases with each verb.

A: *You can check your e-mails.*

check   B: *And your homework.*

C: *And you can check the time. That's three!*

5 (1.24) Listen and read the dialogue. Find and correct seven more mistakes.

Sandra: Hi, Ben! Where are you?

Ben: Oh, hi, Sandra. I'm in ~~Pete's~~ *Jack's* Café.

Sandra: Are you eating a sandwich?!

Ben: No, I'm not! I'm drinking a cup of tea!

Sandra: Is Fiona there, too?

Ben: Yes. She's working on her laptop.

Sandra: I don't believe you! She's reading a newspaper.

Ben: OK! You're right! Are you at work?

Sandra: No, I'm at the station. I'm sitting on the train. It's late again. Can I talk to Fiona?

Ben: Sorry. She's talking to her boyfriend on her phone right now.

Sandra: OK. Say hello from me. Bye.

1C 6 Complete the sentences.

1 My children get a lot of _____ money every week.

2 When I go shopping, I usually pay _____ credit card.

3 Is there a _____ machine near the college?

4 Can I pay by cheque? I'm afraid I don't have any _____ at the moment.

5 We don't have any money. We're _____ !

6 A lot of shops give _____ to students, but they want to see an ID card.

7 Come to the _____ with me on Saturday. Everything's half price.

8 Can you give me some _____ for the ticket machine?

7 Write a sentence about money like the ones in Exercise 6. Leave a gap in your sentence for a partner to complete.

1D 8 (1.25) Choose five words from Word Bank 4, p. 67. Listen and play BINGO! Tick (✓) the words you hear and say *Bingo!* when you have all five.

9 In pairs, write as many clothes as you can in one minute. Look again at Word Bank 4, p. 67.

10 Complete the dialogue with the sentences, A–E.

A: Good morning. (1) _____?

B: Yes. I'm looking for some trainers.

A: Well, we have lots. (2) _____?

B: About £80.

A: Fine. Do you like these ones?

B: Yes. They're nice. (3) _____?

A: Sure. Try these ones, too.

B: Thanks.

A: OK ... Are they OK?

B: Yes, they're fine. (4) _____?

A: Those ones are £75.

B: Great. (5) _____!

A Can I try them on?

B I'll take them.

C Can I help you?

D How much do you want to spend?

E How much are they?

1E **11** Puzzle. Complete the places.

1 Some people go here on Sundays. c _ _ _ _ _

2 You can buy many different things here.

s _ _ _ _ _ _ _ _ _

3 You go here if you're ill. h _ _ _ _ _ _ _

4 You can read books here. l _ _ _ _ _ _

5 You can use this to travel around big cities.

u _ _ _ _ _ _ _ _ _ _

6 You can find a lot of different shops here.

s _ _ _ _ _ _ _ c _ _ _ _ _

7 You can buy a newspaper here.

n _ _ _ _ _ _ _ _ _

8 People live in these

b _ _ _ _ _ of f _ _ _ _

12 Write a puzzle clue about places like the ones in Exercise 11. Leave lines for a partner to complete.

Go to Writing 1 p. 60 ▶

1F **13** Circle the correct option.

1 There aren't *a / any* cash machines in this road.

2 There's *a / any* taxi outside the hotel.

3 There isn't *a / any* museum near the river.

4 Have you got *a / any* money for the driver?

5 The Tourist Information Office hasn't got *a / any* maps.

6 Can you buy me *a / any* newspaper, please?

7 Are there *a / any* students in the café?

14 Read the text in a minute and circle the correct option below.

US Presidents usually *have got / haven't usually got* a lot in their pockets.

What has George W. Bush got in his pockets?

Has he got (1)_____ mobile? (2)_____ gun? Has he got (3)_____ money or chewing gum? Or just his hands, perhaps?

No! The answer is he hasn't got (4)_____ lot! When (5)_____ Argentinian reporter asked President Bush 'What do you carry in your pockets?, his answer was: 'only (6)_____ white handkerchief. That's all, no money, no wallet, nothing else!'

He hasn't got (7)_____ cash, because his assistants buy everything he wants. He hasn't got (8)_____ mobile, because his staff dial all his calls. He hasn't got (9)_____ house keys because he never opens doors, and he hasn't got (10)_____ car keys because he's got (11)_____ driver – who is also (12)_____ member of the secret service!

15 Read the text again and complete with *a / an* or *any*.

Were you at home yesterday?

Speaking

1 Read the TV guide and answer the questions.

    1 What kind of TV programme is *Superminds*?

    A soap opera / A game show / A news programme

    2 How often do you watch this type of programme? Which one(s)?

    3 Do you have a favourite TV show? Which one(s)?

    4 Would you like to be on a show like *Superminds*?

2 Match the items and the photos, A–E. In pairs, think of another famous example of each.

    [D] a space traveller

    [   ] a famous band

    [   ] a news programme

    [   ] a police investigation

    [   ] a recent biography

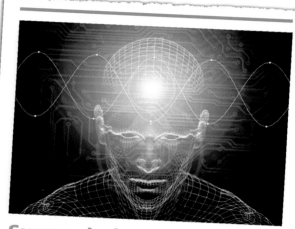

Superminds

Do you think quickly? Can you remember names, places and dates well? Can you sing old songs? Do you follow the lives of famous celebrities?

If your answer to these questions is 'yes', be sure to watch *Superminds* – it's just for you!

Mondays – 21.00 Channel 13

Listening

3 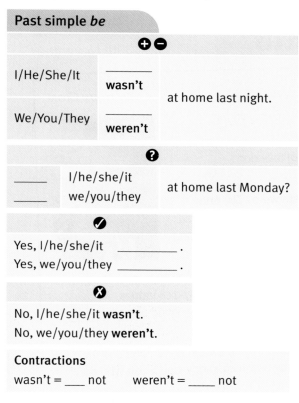(2.1) Listen to *Superminds* and number the photos, A–E, in order, 1–5.

1 ___ **2** ___ **3** ___ **4** ___ **5** ___

Grammar

4 Read the audioscript (2.1) on page 108. Complete the Grammar box with *was* or *were*. What are the four possible answers to *Were you ...?*

Past simple *be*

	⊕ ⊖	
I/He/She/It	——— **wasn't**	at home last night.
We/You/They	——— **weren't**	

	❓	
_____ _____	I/he/she/it we/you/they	at home last Monday?

✔	
Yes, I/he/she/it	_____ .
Yes, we/you/they	_____ .

✘	
No, I/he/she/it **wasn't**.	
No, we/you/they **weren't**.	

Contractions
wasn't = ___ not   weren't = ____ not

AB, p. 86. Ex. 2 ▶

Pronunciation

5 (2.2) Listen and copy the rhythm. Stress the **pink** words. Then answer the questions.

Heath was an actor. Was he American? No, he wasn't.

David wasn't a Beatle.

Diana was a princess. Was she British? Yes, she was.

Where were Diana and Dodi? They were in Paris. They weren't in London.

Were they in an accident? Yes, they were.

1 Are *was* and *were* usually stressed or unstressed?

2 How do we usually pronounce *was* and *were*?
  a in positive sentences and questions?
  b in negative sentences?
  c in short answers?

Speaking

6 Match the categories and the places, 1–10.

H at home
W at work
E entertainment
S services
ST studying

1 [H] in bed
2 [ ] in class
3 [ ] in a meeting
4 [ ] in a café / restaurant
5 [ ] in the park / garden
6 [ ] at school / university
7 [ ] at a party
8 [ ] at the airport / station
9 [ ] at the beach / cinema / gym
10 [ ] at the hairdresser's / supermarket

Tip

We don't use **the** for **bed**, **class** and **school** because they're 'routine' activities.

7 In pairs or groups, ask and answer. Try to find times, dates and places in common.

A: *Where were you ...?*

yesterday	morning, afternoon, evening, night

last	Monday, night, weekend, week, month, July, year

in	July 2008

on	the 1st, 2nd, 3rd Monday (morning) New Year's Eve

at	8.30 midnight

B: *I was ... . / I don't know. / I don't remember.*

2B There was no internet in the 1970s

Speaking

1 ▢ Get a card from your teacher. In pairs, find five similarities and five differences. Use *There isn't a / an … / There are(n't) … .*

Reading

2 (2.3) Read and listen to Harry's composition in the school magazine and answer the questions.

Composition of the month

30th November

Different generations, different technology!

by Harry Grant

My grandparents are funny people. They often tell me: 'You're very young, there's a lot you don't know.'

OK, I'm still at school. But there are lots of things I know that they don't, because our worlds are completely different.

5 When I was born – in 1993 – there was satellite TV and there were CDs, and my grandparents were OK with them. But there wasn't a computer in our house. For them, a *mouse* was just an animal, *windows* were part of the house, *chatting* was talking to the neighbours, and a *web* was just something for spiders!

There was no broadband for the internet – imagine life without it! There were no DVDs, mobiles or 10 MP3 players! The words *e-mail, CD-ROM, iPod* and *memory stick* weren't in any dictionaries. Grandpa and Grandma think they know a lot. But they know nothing of my new world of digital technology.

I understand it very well. They don't. For me, the real difference between the old generation and the new one today is not age. It's between those people who enjoy new technology, and those who don't 15 have any idea about it!

1 What does Harry do?

2 How old is he?

3 Who or what do the words in green refer to?

   'They' (line 1) refers to his grandparents.

4 Do you agree with Harry about the difference between generations?

3 Harry's world or his grandparent's world? Write H (Harry) or G (his grandparents). Some can be both.

1 ___ the internet

2 ___ a mouse

3 ___ an e-mail

4 ___ windows

5 ___ a CD-ROM and DVDs

6 ___ a web

7 ___ CDs

8 ___ a mouse

9 ___ satellite TV

10 ___ windows

11 ___ a computer in the house

12 ___ the web

Grammar

4 Complete the Grammar box with the yellow sentences from Harry's text. Which word means 'not a' or 'not any'?

there was / there were	
singular	**plural**
➕ There was satellite TV.	_____
➖ There was no broadband.	_____
_____	There weren't any PCs in the 1980s.
⦸ Was there wifi 20 years ago?	Were there VCRs when you were a child?
⦸ Yes, **there was.** / No, **there wasn't.**	Yes, **there were.** / No, **there weren't.**

AB, p. 87. Ex. 2 ▶

5 Write true sentences with *there was / wasn't / were / weren't*. In pairs, compare sentences.

1 When I was a child / MP3 players.

2 In 1985 / simple video games.

3 15 years ago / text messaging.

4 / internet in the 1990s.

5 / music CDs in the 1970s.

6 / digital cameras in the 1980s.

Speaking

6 Match five of the items, A–I and the photos, 1–5.

A the first automatic washing machines

B the first cheap colour TVs and microwaves

C stereo radio and the first commercial dishwashers

D wireless internet / wifi

E the first domestic air conditioning

F the first electric irons and vacuum cleaners

G the first laptops and digital cameras

H the first personal stereos and commercial e-mails

I the first rock 'n' roll records

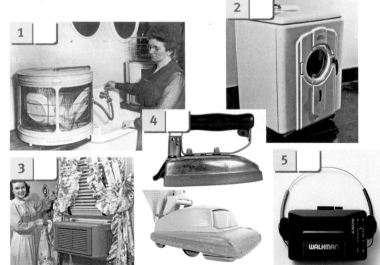

7 (2.4) In pairs, put items A–I from Exercise 6 on the timeline. Listen and check. Were there any surprises?

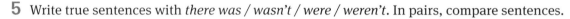

| 1920s | 1930s | 1940s | 1950s | 1960s | 1970s | 1980s | 1990s | 2000s |

8 In pairs, use the phrases in the box to ask questions and make true sentences. Any surprises?

A: *Were there any digital cameras when you were at school?*

B: *I know that in the 1970s, there were no mobile phones.*

When I was a child, … .
(Ten) years ago, … .
When you were at school, … .
… in the (1970s).
… in (1996).

Sen needed to go to Beijing

Listening

1 (2.5) Listen and number the pictures 1–7 in the order you hear them.

A *Yesterday*

Can ... the next flight to Beijing?

B *Then*

Taxi! ... please. I'm in a hurry!

C

Thanks ... Keep the change!

D *and then*

Thank ... boarding card. Gate 17.

E *But*

Oh ... hour late – again!

F *Finally*

Good ... boarding card, please?

G

Good ...
... be late!

2 In pairs, try to remember the five missing words for each picture. Listen again and check.

3 (2.6) Match these verbs and the pictures, A–G, from Exercise 1. Listen and check.

- [ ] arrive (at the airport)
- [ ] board (a plane)
- [ ] book (a ticket)
- [ ] check in (for a flight)
- [ ] hurry (to a meeting)
- [ ] stop (a taxi)
- [ ] wait (for an hour)

Pronunciation

4 (2.7) Listen and repeat each verb phrase in the past tense. Then answer the questions.

1 Are any of the verbs pronounced –ed /ed/ ?

2 How is the pronunciation of *wait* and *board* in the past different from the other five?

Grammar

5 Read the text and look at the verbs. How do we make the past tense in English? Complete the Grammar box.

> Last week, Sen booked a ticket for the next flight to Beijing. Then he stopped a taxi. He arrived at the airport and then he checked in. But he waited for an hour because the plane was late. Finally, he boarded the plane and hurried to the meeting. He was very late!

Past simple regular verbs

To form the past tense, add _ _.
book + _ _ = book**ed**
arrive – ̶e̶ + **ed** = _ _ _ _ _ _ _
hurry – ̶y̶ + **i** + **ed** = _ _ _ _ _ _ _
stop + **p** + _ _ = stop**ped**

There's only one positive form for all persons.

For –*ed* endings, only verbs ending in the sound *t* or *d* add an extra syllable, /ɪd/:

want – wanted, need – needed

In all other verbs, the *e* is silent:

worked, lived, played, changed, married

AB, p. 88. Ex. 2 ▶

6 (2.8) Complete the sentences with a verb in the box in the past. Listen and check.

die   end   host   invent   reunite   start   walk

> **Key dates of the last 75 years**
>
> 1 The Second World War _____ in September 1939 and _____ in August 1945.
>
> 2 Mahatma Gandhi _____ in New Delhi on 30th January 1948.
>
> 3 In 1959, Jack Kilby _____ the first silicon chip in Dallas, Texas.
>
> 4 Neil Armstrong _____ on the Moon on 21st July 1969.
>
> 5 In 1990, East and West Germany _____ .
>
> 6 China _____ the Olympic Games in Beijing in August 2008.

Speaking

7 In pairs, look at Sen's story in Exercise 5.

1 A: Close your book. Tell the story from memory.
B: Listen and help with any words A forgets.
Swap roles.

2 Now act out the story:
B: You're Sen. Remember his words and act.
A: You're the narrator. Tell the story after B acts and says it.
Swap roles.

B: *Can I have a ticket for the next flight to Beijing?*

A: *Last week, Sen booked a ticket for the next flight to Beijing.*

8 Write seven true sentences. Then find somebody with a similar sentence to you for each one.

Begin with:
When I was a child, ...

I wanted to be ...	I enjoyed studying ...
I played ...	I loved ...
I watched ... on TV	I hated ...
I listened to ...	

> *When I was a child, I wanted to be a dancer.*

His life was an opera

Reading

1 (2.9) Think of three key dates in your life. Word Bank 7, p. 70.

2 What do you know about Pavarotti? Write T (true), F (false) or ? (I don't know).

1 He was from Madrid in Spain. ____
2 He studied music at university. ____
3 He worked with the Four Tenors. ____
4 He sang at four World Cups. ____

5 He was only famous in the West. ____
6 He worked a lot for charity. ____
7 He was married three times. ____
8 He died of cancer in Italy in 2008. ____

3 (2.10) Listen to and read his biography to check your answers. What else did you learn from the text?

Luciano Pavarotti was born on 12th October 1935 in Modena, Italy. He first worked as a primary school teacher. An amateur singer, he only studied music at the age of 19 after Arrigo Pola, a famous teacher, heard his beautiful voice. Arrigo trained him for free because Luciano didn't have any money.

He became a professional opera singer and went all over Europe. His first concert as the Three Tenors (with Plácido Domingo and José Carreras) at the 1990 Italian World Cup made him an international star. They sang at the World Cups in Los Angeles, Paris and Yokohama, too, and made opera universally popular.

He gave many spectacular concerts in every continent. Half a million people saw him in New York's Central Park on 26th June 1993 and millions more watched on TV. He sold more records than any classical musician. He raised many millions for charities, too, often singing with pop stars like Eric Clapton and U2.

Luciano was 1.84 m tall and loved cooking, eating, horse-riding, football and women. He had four daughters, two wives and a granddaughter.

He got ill in his 60s but never stopped singing. He died of cancer on 6th September 2007 in Modena. His friend Bono said, 'Some can sing opera, Luciano Pavarotti was an opera. He lived the songs …'

4 Match the yellow words in the text with the definitions.

1 When a person speaks or sings, you hear their _____ .
2 An adjective which means 'high'. _____
3 An adjective meaning 'dramatic and fantastic to see'. _____
4 Without asking for any money. _____

5 The opposite of 'professional'. _____
6 The place where you study from the age of five. _____
7 An adverb which means 'everywhere'. _____

Grammar

5 (2.11) Find 12 verbs in the text in Exercise 3 to complete the Grammar box. Listen, check and repeat.

Past tense irregular verbs

become	_ _ _ _ _ _	give	_ _ _ _	hear	_ _ _ _ _ _	see	_ _ _
do(n't)	_ _ _(n't)	go	_ _ _ _	make	_ _ _ _	sell	_ _ _ _
get	_ _ _	have	_ _ _	say	_ _ _ _	sing	_ _ _ _

Past simple verbs have only one form, except **be**, which has two: _____ and _____ .

AB, p. 89. Ex. 2 ▶

Pronunciation

6 Are the vowel sounds in these verbs the same (S) or different (D)?

1 gave / made _S_
2 had / became _D_
3 did / said ___
4 sang / had ___
5 got / was ___

6 heard / were ___
7 saw / got ___
8 made / sang ___
9 said / went ___
10 got / sold ___

Speaking

7 (2.12) In pairs, look again at Word Bank 7. Tell Bella's 'story' in the past. Listen and check.

Bella was born on … . She … . She … when she was …

8 Write your timeline. Choose five important dates. Use the ideas in Exercise 1.

19...

I was born

9 Tell your partner about your life.

I was born in 19 … . In … , I … .

10 Memory test! Tell your partner his or her biography.

You were born in 19 … . In … , you … .

That's right. or No, sorry. That's wrong.

They didn't sing together

Speaking

1 Complete the musicians' names with vowels and match them to a photo, A–C. What do you know about them?

1 B _ b M _ rl _ y _ nd th _ W _ _ l _ rs

2 Q _ _ _ n

3 P _ nk Fl _ yd

B

A

C

Listening

2 (2.13) Listen to Ali and Max. Who's the Freddie Mercury fan?

3 Listen again and complete the dialogue with the words in the box.

> all right   great   incredible   political
> wonderful   young   much

Ali: What do you think of Queen?

Max: I love them. They're (1)_____. And you?

Ali: They're OK. That Eddy Mercury – he was (2)_____ .

Max: You mean Freddie Mercury. He wrote (3)_____ songs. And had an (4)_____ voice! I loved him.

Ali: Yeah, but I didn't like him very (5)_____ .

Max: No? Why not?

Ali: His songs were, you know, um, very (6)_____ – especially *Another Brick in the Wall*.

Max: But he didn't sing that! That was Pink Floyd, not Queen!

Ali: Really?

Max: Don't you know anything about music?

Ali: Oops ... Sorry. I guess *I'm* too (7)_____.

Grammar

4 (2.14) Link the words and expressions to make four true sentences. Listen, check and repeat.

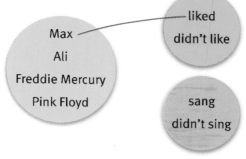

5 Complete the Grammar box with sentences from Exercise 4.

Past simple (➕➖)

➕ _____
_____

➖ *Ali didn't like Freddie Mercury.*
_____

For regular and irregular verbs, use ***didn't* + infinitive** for all persons.

Contractions
didn't = did not

AB, p. 90. Ex. 2 ▶

6 (2.15) Listen and circle ten mistakes in the text.

Bob Marley was born in Jamaica on 6th February 1945. He was a jazz singer and songwriter, and he wrote that famous song *Imagine*. He played the drums. In the 1960s and 1970s, he worked with the Beatles, and he sang with Freddie Mercury, too. Bob Marley had three children. He didn't smoke and he loved playing tennis. He died of AIDS in a Miami hospital at the age of 37. He gave jazz a universal audience.

7 In pairs, correct the mistakes. Which Bob Marley songs do you know?

Bob Marley wasn't a jazz singer. He was a reggae singer.

Speaking

8 Use five of the verbs in the box to make negative past sentences, true or false. In groups, guess what's true or false.

see   go to   meet   get   play   write   do

A: *I didn't see a film yesterday.*

B: *I think that's true. And you?*

C: *No, I think that's false. I think she saw a film yesterday! OK?*

B: *OK. We think it's false. Are we right?*

2f Did you have a good weekend?

Pronunciation

1 (2.16) What's the first sound in each word in the lesson title? Word Bank 8A, p. 71.

Did = /d/

Listening

2 (2.17) Listen and read the dialogue and cross out the extra word in each line.

Tom:	Hi, Mel. Did you have a ~~really~~ good weekend?
Mel:	No way, I didn't. It was terrible …
Tom:	Why not? What did you do?
Mel:	Well, I went to the cinema on Saturday … But then I came to work on Sunday!
Tom:	What? Why did you do that? Are you crazy? We don't usually work at weekends …
Mel:	I know! I thought it was Monday. I left home very early and came to the meeting.
Tom:	Oh, no! I don't believe it! You forgot the BIG meeting!
Mel:	Of course not! I just got the wrong day, that's all. The meeting's this morning!
Tom:	Mel, it's 10.30 now!! The meeting started over an hour ago!
Mel:	No! What's wrong with me? Maybe I *am* going crazy?

3 Read the dialogue again and tick (✓) the correct option.

1 Did Mel have a good weekend?

☐ Yes, she did.   ☐ No, she didn't.

2 Did she need to work on Sunday?

☐ Yes, she did.   ☐ No, she didn't.

3 What time did the meeting start?

☐ At 9.30.   ☐ At 10.30.

4 What mistake(s) did she make?

☐ The wrong day   ☐ The wrong time   ☐ Both

Grammar

4 Read the dialogue in Exercise 2 again. In pairs, answer the questions.

1 Underline nine different verbs in the past. What are their infinitives?

2 Why does Mel say *came to work / came to the meeting* and not *went*? What's the difference between *come* and *go*?

> **Tip**
>
> *Come* means 'in the direction of the speaker or listener':
> *Come here!*
>
> *Go* means 'away from' the speaker or listener:
> *Go home!*

5 Look at the dialogue again and the questions in Exercise 3. Complete the Grammar box.

> **Past simple (?)**
>
> What _____ you **do** last weekend?
> I **went** to the cinema.
>
> What time _____ it **start**?
> It **started** at nine o'clock.
>
> **Did** you / she **have** a good weekend?
> Yes, I / she _____ . No, I/she _____ .
>
> In questions, use ***did*** and **infinitive** for all persons.

Listening

6 (2.18) Mel asks Tom about his weekend. Listen and tick (✓) the correct answers.

	Friday	Saturday	Sunday
Tom went out	☐	☐	☐
Tom stayed in	☐	☐	☐

7 Listen again and number Tom's activities in order, 1–6.

☐ be online   ☐ study for a test
☐ cook a meal   ☐ tidy the flat
☐ go for a run   ☐ watch TV

Speaking

8 (2.19) Listen and repeat Mel's six questions. How do we usually pronounce *did you*?

Did you *have a good weekend?*

9 Think about the three nights of last weekend. In pairs, look at the chart.
 A: Make sure you can ask all the questions. Each ✳ = one missing word.
 B: Prepare your answers to the questions. Think of one or two more things you can say, too.

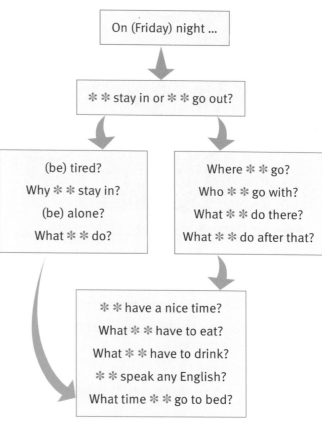

What did you do last weekend?

On (Friday) night ...

✳ ✳ stay in or ✳ ✳ go out?

(be) tired?
Why ✳ ✳ stay in?
(be) alone?
What ✳ ✳ do?

Where ✳ ✳ go?
Who ✳ ✳ go with?
What ✳ ✳ do there?
What ✳ ✳ do after that?

✳ ✳ have a nice time?
What ✳ ✳ have to eat?
What ✳ ✳ have to drink?
✳ ✳ speak any English?
What time ✳ ✳ go to bed?

10 In pairs, ask and answer about last weekend.
 A: Look at the chart and ask the questions.
 B: Close your book, look at A and answer the questions. Swap roles. Were your weekends similar?

A: *We both stayed in on Friday night, but only one of us went out on Saturday night.*

Go to **Phrasebook 2** p. 77 ▶   Go to **Essential Grammar 2** p. 114 ▶

Revision

2A 1 Complete the sentences with *in*, *on* or *at*.

1 Paolo's not very well. He's _____ bed.

2 Why wasn't Gina _____ work yesterday?

3 We have two English lessons _____ Tuesdays.

4 Pete and Denise were _____ the cinema last night.

5 The film starts _____ 6.30.

6 I wasn't _____ home yesterday afternoon.

7 My friends are _____ work today.

8 Is your birthday _____ 8th March?

2 Write true sentences for each line. Use a different person and place for each.
Give them to a partner to check for you.

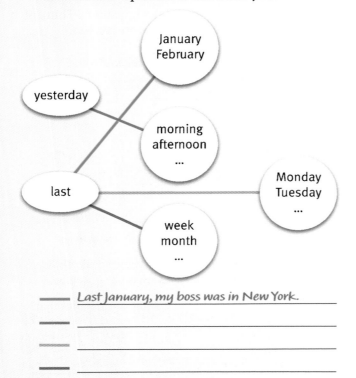

_____ *Last January, my boss was in New York.*

_____ _____

_____ _____

_____ _____

2B 3 (2.20) Listen to Chris talking about his first job. Correct the sentences.

1 Chris was a chef.

2 There weren't any waitresses.

3 There were ten tables inside and ten tables outside.

4 It was a French café.

5 The food was expensive.

6 There was a map on the wall.

7 Chris works in Paris now.

4 Write five sentences about your first school. In pairs, compare answers. How many things were the same?

A: *There wasn't a white board. It was black!*

B: *There weren't any computers in the school.*

2C 5 In pairs, write a quiz about famous people. Think of five questions.

1 *She played Evita Peron in the film* Evita.

2 *He painted the Mona Lisa.*

2D 6 Circle the correct option.

1 My parents *got / became* married in 1985.

2 They *had / went* abroad every year for their summer holiday.

3 They *did / had* their first baby 20 years ago – me!

4 I *graduated / left* from university at the end of July.

5 I *went / started* school when I was four years old.

6 My brother *got / made* his first job on a TV show last year.

7 He *gave / got* his first car when he was 18.

7 In pairs, talk about when important events in your life happened.

I graduated from university two years ago.

8 Read and complete the verbs in this biography of Freddie Mercury.

Freddie Mercury was born in Zanzibar on 5th September 1946. His real name (1)w_ _ Farrokh Bulsara. His parents (2)we_ _ Indian and he (3)ha_ one sister, Kashmira.

Mercury (4)we_ _ to school in Mumbai, India. At school he (5)lik_ _ boxing and playing the piano. When he (6) w_ _ 17, his family (7)mov_ _ to London. At university, he (8)stud_ _ _ Art and after that he (9)work_ _ at Heathrow airport before he (10)start_ _ the band Queen, with Brian May and Roger Taylor in 1970.

He (11)w_ _ a great singer and (12) ha_ an incredible voice. He (13)wro_ _ many famous songs, including *We Are the Champions*. His last concert (14)w_ _ on August 9th 1986 in front of 300,000 people. He never (15)marr_ _ _ and (16)di_ _ of AIDS on November 24 1991 at the age of 45.

9 Read about three people's weekends. In pairs, say which weekends were similar to yours. What was similar / different to you?

Ally: I didn't go out on Saturday. I watched some TV, listened to music and studied for a test. On Sunday morning, I met some friends and we went to the beach. We stayed there all day. I was very tired in the evening, so I went to bed early.

Brian: On Saturday morning, my wife and I went swimming, and in the evening, we had dinner at a Chinese restaurant. Then we went to a party. It was great!

We were tired on Sunday, so we spent the day reading and in the evening, we played cards with some friends.

Celine: I didn't do anything on Saturday. I stayed in all day. It was very boring! But on Sunday I played tennis in the morning, I saw an excellent film in the afternoon, and then I went dancing with my boyfriend in the evening.

A: *My weekend was similar to Ally's and to Celine's, because I stayed in on Saturday, but I didn't watch TV.*

B: *I went to … , but I didn't …*

10 In pairs, think about what you did last night.
A: Tell your partner what you did last night.
B: Ask two questions about each thing A did.

A: *I watched TV.*

B: *What programme did you watch? What time did it start?*

11 Get cards from your teacher. Read about John Lennon. Ask and answer questions to complete the text.

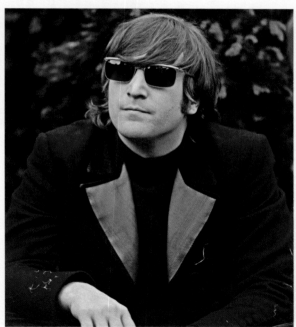

Song: *And I love her* by The Beatles

To find the words, google lyric + the name of the song.

To find the video, google video + the name of the song and singer.

Go to Writing 2 p. 61 ▶

Images

Speaking

1 Answer the questionnaire. In pairs, compare answers. Who's more into photography?

> ### Are you into photography?
>
> **1** Do you have a (digital) camera? How often do you use it / them?
> **2** When do you take photos?
> **3** Where do you keep your pictures?
> **4** Do you like to print out photos? Why / Why not?
> **5** Do you carry photos with you? Why / Why not?
> **6** Do you have any photos in your room at home? Which ones?
> **7** Which is your favourite photo at the moment? Why?

2 Look at the photos for a minute, then cover them. In pairs, remember all you can.

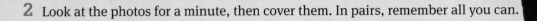

A: *There are lots of trees and boats.*

Listening

3 (3.1) Dana sent Toni a photo. Listen and answer.

1 Who calls who?
2 What's the problem?
3 Is this Mayflower Gardens or Jupiter Park?

4 Listen again. What are the five differences between the photo Toni has and the one you can see?

Pronunciation

5 (3.2) Complete the Grammar Box. Can you pronounce the irregular plurals? Word Bank 8B, p. 71.

| Irregular plurals | |
Singular	Plural
a man	_____
a woman /ˈwʊmən/	_____ /ˈwɪmɪn/
a child /tʃaɪld/	_____
a person /ˈpɜːsən/	_____ /ˈpiːpəl/

6 Listen again to Dani and Toni. How do they combine these sentences?

1 There are families. They're relaxing in a park.

There are _____ .

2 There's a young guy. He's playing the guitar.

There's _____ .

3 There's a man. He's standing by a tree.

There _____ .

4 There are two children. They're playing with a ball.

There _____ .

Grammar

7 Complete the Grammar box.

Linking ideas, present and past	
There's a girl.	**There__** a girl _____ a hotdog.
She**'s eating** a hotdog.	
There are lots of people.	**There** ____ lots of people _____ to work.
They**'re driving** to work.	
There were some children.	**There** ____ some children _____ .
They **were sleeping**.	

AB, p. 93. Ex. 3 ▶

8 Look again at the cartoon on page 8 and 9. Make four sentences similar to the Grammar box.

There's a man wearing a grey uniform and

brown shoes.

Reading

9 Do you know what *Flickr* is?
Read and answer the questions.

1 What can users share, keep and create there?

2 What can photographers write to go with their postcards?

flickr

Flickr is a photo-sharing website. It's also an online community platform. Users can share personal photographs, and many bloggers keep their photos here, too.

With Flickr, you can create your own postcards. There are all types of pictures from every continent! The postcards include a picture plus a short comment, story or message from the photographer.

10 Read the bubble and comment for the first photo. In pairs, write a bubble and comment for three photos in this lesson. Swap with another pair and match them with the photos.

I'm freezing!

This is a picture of me and my children skiing in Switzerland.

How much exercise do you do?

Speaking

1 In pairs, ask and answer.

1 How often do you feel stressed?

2 Name three things which stress you.

3 When was the last time you felt stressed?

4 How do you fight stress?

5 Do you think stress is a big danger for health?

Reading

2 (3.3) Listen and read the article. Underline any words with difficult pronunciation. Find:

1 five problems caused by stress

2 four ways to fight stress

Stress: a serious danger!
'It's probably just stress.' 'It's nothing serious.'

How often do you hear (or say) this when people have a minor health problem? But stress is not just 'minor'. The American Medical Association says stress is very serious and can be a major danger to health. It can cause heart attacks, depression and cancer. Stress can also stop you sleeping and causes bad habits, like eating a lot, smoking and drinking too much.

Doing exercise is a great way to fight stress. But for some people, simple activities can also help a lot, like playing with children, watching a favourite TV show or taking a hot bath. The AMA says it is essential to focus on fighting stress every day, and not just at weekends.

3 Read aloud the sentences 1–10 in the quiz in Exercise 4. Pronounce the pink letters in *at*, *about* and *of* as /ə/. How do you pronounce items A–E?

A
B
C
D
E

4 (3.4) Do the quiz, then listen and check your answers. How many did you get right?

A healthy body and mind: what's true and what's false?
A quiz by Jill Woods, M.D., author of *Live Well*.

Do you know what's good for you? Write ✓ ✗ = in the boxes
✓ **It's good advice.**   ✗ **It's bad advice.**   = **It makes no difference.**

1 Drink about six glasses of water a day. ☐
2 Sleep at least eight hours a day. ☐
3 Have at least three meals a day. ☐
4 Read about two books a month. ☐
5 Watch about two good films a month. ☐
6 Eat a box of chocolates a week. ☐
7 Drink a cup of coffee a day. ☐
8 Do exercise once a week. ☐
9 Have a bottle of wine with dinner every evening. ☐
10 Smoke a packet of cigarettes a week. ☐

---

5 Are you a healthy pair? Ask your partner the ten quiz questions.

A: *Do you drink …?*

B: *Yes, … . / No, … .*

Listening

6 (3.5) Kate's asking Leo about his health. Listen, answer and check in pairs.

1 Does Leo think he's healthy?

2 Does Anna agree with all Leo's answers?

3 Does Leo drink alcohol and smoke?

4 Did Leo enjoy the conversation?

Grammar

7 Listen again. Read and circle the correct option.

Kate: Are you a healthy person, Leo?

Leo: Of course! Very!

Kate: Are you sure? How much ⁽¹⁾*work / exercise* do you do?

Anna: Very little.

Leo: Anna! Um, some, but, er, not a lot ...

Kate: Hmmm ... I see. How much ⁽²⁾*coffee / water* do you drink a day?

Anna: Litres and litres ...

Leo: At least three ⁽³⁾*cups / times* a day, I think.

Kate: OK. And how many ⁽⁴⁾*stories / books* do you read a month?

Leo: None! I don't have time to read, you know.

Kate: Really? How much ⁽⁵⁾*wine / alcohol* do you drink, Leo?

Leo: I sometimes drink one or two ⁽⁶⁾*glasses / cups* of wine at dinner ...

Anna: No, you don't! Come on, Leo! You drink a ⁽⁷⁾*glass / bottle* of wine a day! Especially when you're cooking!

Tim: And how many ⁽⁸⁾*packets / cigarettes* do you smoke a day, Leo?

Anna: He smokes a lot! He bought three packets yesterday!

Leo: But I only smoked four. Come on, guys, please!

8 Complete the Grammar box with *much* or *many*.

How much / How many?	
How _____ exercise ...? coffee ...?	**None.** (= no exercise) **Some.** (= not a lot) / Three cups.
How _____ books ...? cups of coffee ...?	**None.** (= no books) **Some.** (= not a lot) / Three.
Use **How** _____? with countable nouns (plural form) Use **How** _____? with uncountable nouns (no plural)	

AB, p. 94. Ex. 5 ▶

Speaking

9 Change partners. Ask what your new partner had yesterday. Use *How much* or *How many* and quiz photos A–E. Did you both have healthy days?

A: *How much coffee did you have yesterday?* or *How many cups of coffee ...?*

B: *I think I just had one cup. / None.*

10 Survey. Choose three *How many / How much ...?* questions to ask the class about their habits. Who's very healthy? Who's the 'Leo' of your class?

A: *How much curry do you usually eat a week?*

How much?

How many?

do
eat
have
read
sleep
smoke
watch

3C I can do a lot on a computer!

English@work

1 Are you a good computer user? Match the photos, 1–6, and six of the computer skills, A–K.

Computer skills

A create a spreadsheet

B download music and video files

C have a phone conversation on the internet

D install software

E make a blog / photolog

F prepare a PowerPoint presentation

G upload a video

H use a scanner

I use a messenger

J write and send an e-mail

K type fast

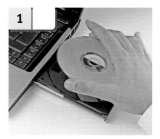

2 In pairs, decide if the computer skills, A–K, are easy, difficult, boring and / or interesting.

A: *I think installing software is boring.*

B: *I agree. I did it last weekend and it's very slow. / I disagree. I think it's … .*

Listening

3 In pairs, read the e-mail and answer the questions.

1 What job is Jo trying to get?

2 Why didn't Tim answer her before?

3 What date is Jo's interview?

4 Which skills from Exercise 1 do you think are important for this job?

> **From:** Tim Grant – *The Planet News* – Editor
> **To:** Jo Tucker
> **Subject:** Job Interview
> **Sent:** Friday, 18 July 10:25
>
> Dear Ms Tucker,
>
> Thank you for your CV and application for the job as my personal assistant.
>
> I'm sorry I couldn't answer you before now, but we had an enormous number of applications, of which yours was certainly one of the best!
>
> Could you please come for an interview next Wednesday, July 23rd

4 (3.6) Listen to part of Tim and Anna's interview with Jo. Write T (true) or F (false).

1 Jo can type quite fast. ___

2 She can't create spreadsheets. ___

3 She can install software very well. ___

4 She can't use a scanner. ___

5 She can prepare PowerPoint presentations very well. ___

6 She could speak Spanish very well five years ago. ___

7 She can write e-mails in Spanish very well. ___

Tip

✓ I can use Vista.

✗ I know to use Vista.

Grammar

5 Study Tim's e-mail and the sentences in Exercise 4. Complete the Grammar box with these words.

> can   can't   Could   could   couldn't   same   Can

can / could

Use **can**

1 to talk about skills: *I can / can't swim (very well).*

2 for requests: *Can / _____ you help me, please?*

Can and **can't** is the _____ for all persons:

? _____ *he / she / they, etc. drive?*

+ *Yes, they _____ . / No, they _____ .*

The question and negative past forms are _____ and _____ .

AB, p. 95. Ex. 3 ▶

Pronunciation

6 (3.7) Listen. In each sentence is *can* stressed (S) or unstressed (U)? Mark *S* or *U*.

ᵁ Can you speak French?	No, but I can speak Spanish quite well.
	Yes, I can.
	No, I can't. Not very well.
	I can't speak French.

Is *can* usually stressed (S) or unstressed (U) in:

	S	U
questions?	☐	☐
positive sentences?	☐	☐
negatives?	☐	☐
short answers?	☐	☐

7 (3.8) Listen. In pairs, answer the five questions. Are you and your partner similar?

8 In pairs, ask and answer about the skills in Exercise 1. Which ones could you do five years ago?

A: *Can you create a spreadsheet?*

B: *Yes, I can now, but I couldn't five years ago. Can you?*

A: *No, I can't. Can you ...?*

Speaking

9 Roleplay: job interview.

A: You're the interviewer. Look at the form and prepare your questions. Can you find a better personal assistant than Jo?

B: You're the interviewee. Look at the form and prepare your answers. What can you do that Jo can't do?

Begin like this:

A: *Come in. Please sit down. Now (Mr Martin), can I ask you some questions?*

Application for job as Personal Assistant to the Editor

Full name: _____

🏠 : _____

_____

☎ : _____

📱 : _____

💻 **Skills:**

🧮 ☐   🎵 ☐   skype ☐   💻 ☐

📱 ☐   ⌨ ☐   ⊚ ☐

Previous office experience:

Yes: ... months ... years   No ☐

Languages:

A = well   B = quite well   C = a little

1 _____	2 _____	3 _____
speak __	speak __	speak __
on the phone __	on the phone __	on the phone __
write e-mails __	write e-mails __	write e-mails __
read texts __	read texts __	read texts __

Interests:

_____

I need to learn quickly

Reading

1 Read the introduction to the web page. Think of six tips to learn English quickly.

Q: I'm studying English at school. But I need to learn quickly. What can I do?

A: To learn very fast – in 30 days for example – is impossible. Learning a language well takes many months. But you can learn more quickly by following these eight tips carefully:

2 In pairs, look at the tips below.

  1 Read the first half of the text in two minutes.
    A: Read tips 1 and 2.
    B: Read tips 3 and 4.
    Tell each other what you can remember.

  2 Read the second half in two more minutes.
    A: Read tips 5 and 6.
    B: Read tips 7 and 8.
    Again, tell each other what you can remember.

  3 How many of your ideas from Exercise 1 aren't in the text?

  4 Which tips do / don't you follow?

  5 Choose a tip which you don't follow well to try before the next class.

---

1 Give yourself time
Do you really want to learn English? <u>It isn't easy</u>, and takes a lot of time. Can you really give that time? If not, no class can help you.

2 Be realistic
Ask yourself: 'What's my goal today? What exactly do I want to practise?' You can't learn English in one day. Focus and give yourself small goals, e.g. try to learn eight new words or phrases every day, six days a week. Then take one day off to celebrate! That's 200 words a month!

3 Feel your progress
Think about where you are today, where you were last month and where you want to be next month. It's important to notice your progress, even if it's only a little. Do lots of exercises and tests, too.

4 Study regularly
Studying 15 minutes a day is 100% better than studying for two hours once a week. 'A little, often' is the best way to remember.

5 Take every opportunity
TV, the internet, tourists … English is everywhere! Always keep something English with you (a text, a recording, some word cards), so <u>you can easily practise</u> when you get five minutes free. Put English phrases on your walls at home, too.

6 Listen a lot
Listening is the most important language skill. Listen to the radio, MTV, films, iPods, the Net, anything. Listening to the same texts again and again really helps pronunciation and memory, too.

7 Don't be afraid to speak
The number-one problem for learners is fear. For example, fear of making mistakes or of looking stupid. The best way to learn <u>anything</u> is to do it – again and again – until you get it right. Don't let a little fear stop you from getting what you want.

8 Don't study alone – have fun!
Speak English with friends when you can. Choose a 'homework partner'. Study together or phone each other when you can't meet. Find an e-pal to practise with, too.

Grammar

3 Complete the Grammar box with yellow words from the two texts (there are two extra yellow words you don't need).

Adjectives	Adverbs
What's a **quick** way to learn?	How can I learn _____?
Practice is **easy**.	You can _____ practise.
What's the **exact** problem?	What _____ is the problem?
Fear is a **real** problem.	Fear is _____ a problem.
Regular study helps.	Studying _____ helps.
I need a **fast** way to learn.	To learn very _____ is impossible!

4 Underline the nouns in the Adjectives column. Underline the verbs in the Adverbs column. Complete the rules and examples.

> **Rules**
>
> 1 Adjectives describe _____ .
>   Adverbs describe _____ .
>
> 2 To form adverbs, we usually add _ _ to the adjective: *badly, slow_ _ , careful_ _* .
>
> 3 Adjectives ending in **–y** → **ɏ** → **–ily**:
>   *easy* → *eas**ily**, happy* → happ_ _ _
>
> 4 These adverbs are irregular:
>   *fast* → _ _ _ _ , *good* → _ _ _ _

AB, p. 96. Ex. 3 ▶

Pronunciation

5 (3.9) Listen and write the five sentences you hear. Underline the four stressed words in each one.

1 *He* _____

2 _____

3 _____

4 _____

5 _____

6 Make four true sentences about you / your family. Use four of the verbs in the box and an adverb. Compare with a partner. Are there any coincidences?

> dance   drive   play   ride a horse   sing   speak

Listening

7 (3.10) Listen and number the pictures, 1–4.

8 Listen again and circle the correct option.

1 By *watch / watching* other people and then *practise / practising* a lot.

2 By *take / taking* lessons. And I'*m study / studied* a lot for the test.

3 I *teach / taught* myself. I *did / made* a lot of mistakes, but I *keep / kept* trying.

4 I *read / bought* lots of cookbooks when I was young. And I often *looked / look* for recipes on the Net.

Speaking

9 Add three skills to the list. In pairs, ask and answer. Tell the class your most interesting answers.

> *cook Chinese food*
> *ride a motorbike*
> *paint pictures*
> _____
> _____

A: *Can you cook English food?*
B: *Yes …*
A: *How did you learn?*

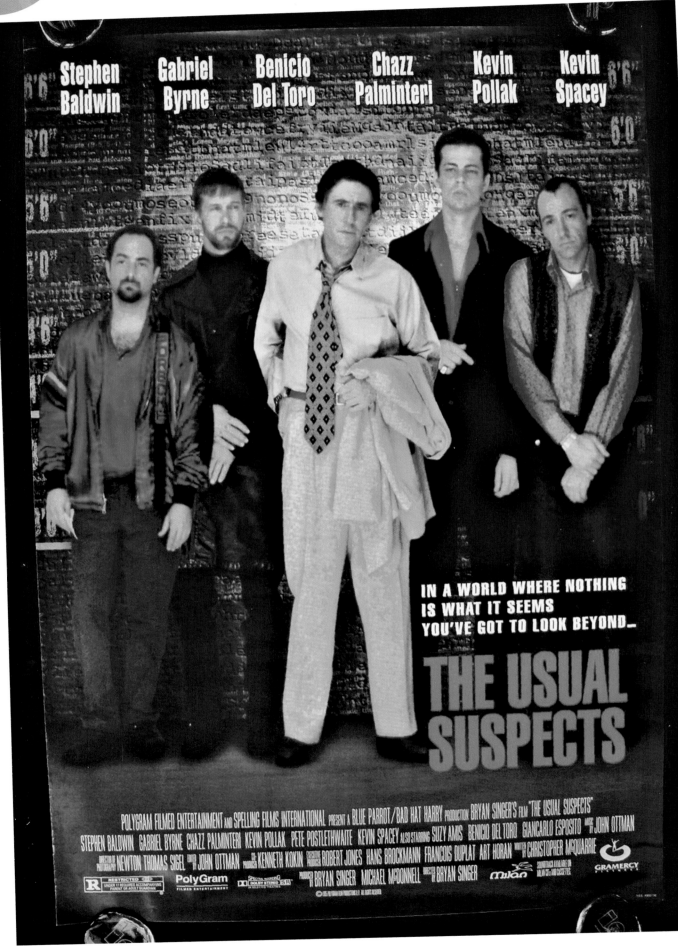

Reading

1 Look at the film poster. In pairs, ask and answer.

1 Do you know this film? Did you enjoy it? Can you remember anything about it?

2 Do you know any of the actors' names?

3 What do you think the word *suspect* means?

4 Close your book. What are the five men are wearing, from left to right?

The first man's wearing … .

2 (3.11) Listen to a film critic talking about the film. What does he think people remember most about the film?

a the acting   c the story

b the photography   d the film poster

3 In pairs, read the review and answer the questions.

The Usual Suspects is one of the best crime thrillers in cinema history. Many people don't remember the film, but they nearly always remember the photo on the film poster. Who can forget the five men in a police line-up looking at the camera? On the left, there is Kevin Pollak, short, bearded and relaxed. Next to him is the attractive but scary Stephen Baldwin, also bearded. In the middle we have the good-looking ex-cop – dark-haired Gabriel Byrne. Next to him is the giant of the group, the tall Benicio Del Toro. And finally, on the right, is Kevin Spacey, looking thin and weak. But don't forget the film itself! The story of five professional criminals is very clever, the acting is excellent, and the directing and photography are brilliant. Don't miss it!

1 Did you name the five actors correctly in Exercise 1?

2 Find words in the text that mean:

a was a police officer before

b people who do bad things

c very tall, large person

d 😲

e not strong

f 😱

g calm

h not forget

4 (3.12) Describe the actors' faces. Word Bank 9, p. 72.

5 Match the descriptions to two of the actors.

1 He's not very young. He's in his thirties. He's not very tall and is of medium build. He's got very short, black hair and I think he's got brown eyes.

2 He's quite young. He's about 28. He's very tall and strong. He's got short, black hair and I think he's got green eyes.

Grammar

6 Complete the Grammar box with *has got*, *have got*, *be* or *'s*. Which noun is uncountable?

Describing people	
She / He	___ (very / quite) young / old, tall / short, thin / fat.
	___ in her / his forties / about 45.
	___ medium height / build.
	___ (nearly) bald.
She / He	_____ (very) long / (quite) short blond(e) hair.
	(quite) a big mouth.
	(brown) eyes / glasses.

Use ___ + adjective or prepositional phrase (e.g. in her / his forties). Use ____ ____ + noun.

AB, p. 97. Ex. 3 ▶

Speaking

7 🗎 Get a card from your teacher.

A: Describe one of the people.

B: Listen and say who it is.

8 In pairs, ask and answer about your family and friends. Are there any surprises?

A: *My mother's quite tall.*

B: *Has she got black hair?*

A: *She had black hair, but it's grey now.*

B: *Is she very thin?*

9 In pairs, practise descriptions.

A: Describe a classmate.

B: Guess who A's describing.

A: *This person's wearing black jeans and a white T-shirt. She's tall and quite thin. She's got short, brown hair and blue eyes.*

B: *Is it Angie?*

Staying at a hotel?

English@work

1 When was the last time you stayed in a hotel? Tell your partner where, why and your opinion of the hotel.

2 Quickly read Pam's e-mail to *USA Today's* travel page. Circle the correct summary, A or B.

  A Pam booked a room, but the hotel was horrible. So she left and went to another one. She wants to know if she can do anything now.

  B Pam booked a room, but when she arrived at the hotel it was full. She couldn't get a hotel room in the city. She wants to know if she can do anything now.

3 Circle the correct option.

  1 A conference is a big *meeting / party*.

  2 A reservation is when you *book / pay for* a room.

  3 A room is available when it is *free / booked*.

  4 A hotel confirms a booking when it *accepts / doesn't accept* it.

  5 You ask for compensation when the problem is *your fault / not your fault*.

  Do you think Pam can do anything now? Why / Why not?

Readers' Letters

Question: Last month I went to Chicago for a conference. I booked a room at the Lodge using their website. They sent me confirmation and I printed it out. I also took a copy of their e-mail confirming my reservation. But when I arrived at the hotel, the staff said there were no rooms available and that there were no rooms in central Chicago! I got really angry when they offered to put me in a hotel outside the city. Is it normal for hotels to confirm a reservation, but not have a room available when you arrive? Can I get compensation?

Pam Vanderwal, Green Bay, Wis.

http://www.usatoday.com

Listening

4 (3.13) Listen to Pam telling Martin about her problem with the hotel. Write T (true) or F (false).

  1 The big hotels overbook by mistake. ____

  2 The same problem happened to Martin. ____

  3 Pam wasn't happy with the hotel she stayed at. ____

  4 Martin's brother got compensation. ____

  5 Martin thinks it's a good idea for Pam to phone the hotel to complain. ____

> **Tip**
> Stress the syllable before *–ion* endings.
>   compensation
>   confirmation
>   expression
>   presentation
>   pronunciation
>   reservation

Grammar

5 (3.14) Read and circle the correct preposition. Listen and check.

Receptionist: Here's the key. You're ⁽¹⁾*in / on* Room 601. Take the elevator ⁽²⁾*to / on* the sixth floor.

Pam: Room 601. ⁽³⁾*To / On* the sixth floor?

Receptionist: That's right. Go ⁽⁴⁾*into / out of* the elevator and turn left. Room 601 is ⁽⁵⁾*on / at* the end ⁽⁶⁾*in / on* the right.

Pam: Thank you. Er, where's the elevator again?

Receptionist: Over there ⁽⁷⁾*to / in* the corner.

Pam: Thanks. See you in a minute.

> **Tip**
>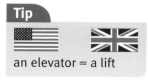
> an elevator = a lift

6 (3.15) Complete the Grammar box with *at*, *in*, *on* or *to*. Listen and check.

(3.16) Word Bank 10, p. 73.

Prepositions

Use ___ , ___ or ___ for position ↓

Use ___ for movement →

Pam's ___ the hotel. ↓

Pam's ___ the elevator. ↓

She's taking the elevator ___ the sixth floor. →

Now she's ___ the sixth floor. ↓

She's walking ___ Room 601. →

Speaking

7 Match the problems and pictures.

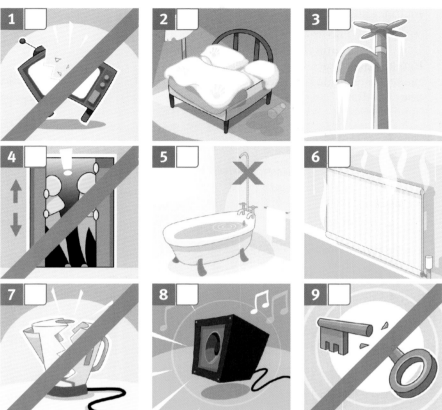

A The kettle didn't work.
B There wasn't a shower.
C I couldn't turn off the heating.
D The room wasn't clean.
E The water wasn't hot.

F The TV didn't work.
G The key didn't work.
H It was very noisy.
I The lift didn't work.

8 (3.17) Pronounce *shower*, *off*, *sixth* and *kettle*. Word Bank 8C, p. 71.

9 (3.18) Listen to the rest of Pam's conversation with Martin. Tick (✓) the six problems in Exercise 7 that Pam had.

10 Complete the conversation with the words in the box.

> sorry   it's   afraid   help   complaint   there

Reception: Hello, reception. How can I (1)_____ you?

Pam: Yes, (2)_____ Pam Vanderwal in Room 601. I've got a (3)_____ . (4)_____ isn't any hot water in the bathroom.

Reception: I'm (5)_____ , Miss Vanderwal. Just wait an hour and try again.

Pam: But I want to have a bath now.

Reception: I'm (6)_____ we have a problem with the water at the moment. Try again in an hour. Thank you, goodbye.

11 In pairs, have short conversations about Pam's other problems.

Go to **Phrasebook 3** p. 78 ▶   Go to **Essential Grammar 3** p. 116 ▶

Revision

3A 1 Get a card from your teacher. Describe your picture and find ten differences.

3B 2 Use the notes and *How much ... ? / How many ... ?* to make questions. Choose three questions and make a questionnaire. Ask the class, then report your results.

Habits questionnaire

1 money / spend every day?

2 cups of coffee / drink?

3 TV programmes / watch in the evening?

4 exercise / do every week?

5 chocolate / eat?

6 time / spend on homework?

7 people / phone every day?

8 time / spend on computer?

9 meals / eat every day?

10 _____ ?

3 3.19 Listen and correct the sentences.

1 Jenny drinks a bottle of water a day.

2 She doesn't do a lot of exercise every week.

3 She doesn't smoke.

4 She has four cups of coffee in the morning.

5 She drinks two glasses of wine with her dinner.

6 She walks in the park with a friend.

3C 4 Get a card from your teacher. Write two more questions. In pairs, ask and answer.

5 Write four sentences with these verb phrases (past or present) that are true for you or someone you know. In pairs, compare your answers. How many are similar?

> walk   talk   read   write   ride a bicycle
> swim   use a computer

A: *My brother could walk when he was nine months old!*

6 Lakeside Holidays need people for this summer. In pairs, carry out interviews.
A: Interview B. Decide if he/she can have the job.
B: You really want to work for Lakeside Holidays.

Lakeside Holidays
need good people – good conditions and salary!

We need:

Office Workers
● use a computer
● install software
● write e-mails

Instructors
● play sports
● play the guitar
● sing
● dance

Counsellors
● work with children
● organise groups
● tell stories

A: *Can you ... ?*

B: *Yes, I can. / No, I can't.*

A: *You can be a(n) ... or a(n) ... / Sorry, you can't work at Lakeside Holidays.*

3D **7** Circle the correct option.

1 Jake drives *quick / quickly*.

2 Mr Jones is a *good / well* teacher.

3 We answered the questions *easy / easily*.

4 I go swimming *regular / regularly*.

5 I prefer *happy / happily* films.

6 The *slow / slowly* train stops at every station.

8 Put the words in order.

1 runs / Mandy / fast / very / .

_____

2 very / sad / hate / films / I / .

_____

3 children / garden / happily / The / played / the / in / .

_____

4 essay / wrote / exam / in / good / the / a / Rod / .

_____

5 is / really / driver / a / slow / Ben / .

_____

6 very / brother / well / My / cooks / .

_____

9 In pairs, talk about what you do slowly or quickly. Use the ideas in the box. What do you have in common?

> eat write type speak run think
> read walk buy things do your homework

A: *I type quickly, but I write slowly.*

3E **10** Correct the mistake in each sentence.

1 Maria has got ✗ dark hair.

2 My uncle has got bald.

3 The actor is of medium tall.

4 Helen is blue eyes.

5 My dad's got beard.

6 The film star has got blue eyes and small face.

Song: *Perfect Day* by Lou Reed

To find the words, google lyric + the name of the song.

To find the video, google video + the name of the song and singer.

Go to **Writing 3** p. 62 ▶

11 Read the text. Do you know who it is?

This week's mystery man was born on 30 January 1974 in Wales, but he lives in Los Angeles now, and people usually think he's American. He has three sisters. As a child, he trained in ballet and guitar before becoming an actor. His many films include Spielberg's *Empire of the Sun*, *American Psycho*, *Batman Begins*, *The Dark Knight* and *Terminator Salvation*.

He has brown hair and green eyes. He's 1m 88 tall and usually has a strong build. But when he acted in the 2004 film, *The Machinist*, he lost 27 kilos and weighed only 55 kilos! On 29 January 2000, he married Sandra Blazic, an ex-model. They have a daughter called Emmeline. He doesn't eat meat and is very interested in animal rights. His initials are CB. Who is he?

12 Game: Play 20 QUESTIONS.

A: Choose a famous person everybody knows (an actor, a teacher, etc.). Answer the questions using only *Yes* or *No*.

Class: You've got 20 questions to guess Student A's person.

Class: *Has she got long hair?*

A: *No, she hasn't.*

3F **13** Complete the e-mail with *in*, *on* or *at*.

Dear Jack

I arrived home yesterday from my holiday. The hotel was great. Thanks for finding it for me (1) _____ the internet. It was (2) _____ the centre of town (3) _____ a quiet street. I could see the city really well because my room was (4) _____ the 10th floor. Ben had an accident (5) _____ the shower (6) _____ the first day and he was (7) _____ hospital for two days, but the doctors were excellent, so that was OK. There was a swimming pool (8) _____ the end of the street, so we went there every day. Oh, and I think we saw Brad Pitt (9) _____ the airport yesterday. I'm sure he looked (10) _____ me!

See you (11) _____ work tomorrow.

Love
Jo

Some women have to wear two hats

Speaking

1 (4.1) What don't you like doing at home? Word Bank 11, p. 74.

2 Read the TV Guide, look at the cover of the book and answer the questions.

1 What type of programme is *Joe's Show*?

2 Who's Sally Welles?

3 What's her book about?

4 What do you think the two 'hats' and two letters, **F** and **P**, mean?

Joe's Show

On the red sofa tonight, Joe Brown chats with best-selling author Sally Welles. Sally's new book, *Wear Two Hats and Be Cool*, discusses women's obligations in the modern world.

Don't miss it! 11 p.m. on Channel 8.

Wear Two Hats and Be Cool

Sally Welles

3 In pairs, decide if activities 1–10 are usually family life (F), professional life (P) or both (B). Circle F, P or B.

1	do housework	F	P	B	☐
2	do the shopping	F	P	B	☐
3	work late	F	P	B	☐
4	prepare meals	F	P	B	☐
5	look after children	F	P	B	☐
6	go to meetings	F	P	B	☐
7	start work early	F	P	B	☐
8	take children to school (the doctor's, the dentist's, etc.)	F	P	B	☐
9	see customers	F	P	B	☐
10	travel on business	F	P	B	☐

Listening

4 (4.2) Listen to Sally. Tick (✓) her obligations on the list in Exercise 3.

5 (4.3) Listen and circle what Sally says.

1 I *have to / don't have to* take the children to school.

2 I *have to / don't have to* see my boyfriend sometimes.

Grammar

6 (4.4) Complete the Grammar box. Listen and repeat. With *have to*, how do we normally pronounce the letters *ve* and the word *to*?

have to (obligations)

➕			
You and I	**have to**		work late.
He	_____ to		

➖			
They	_____ **have to**		get up early.
She	**doesn't** _____ **to**		

❓			
Do	you	**have to**	go home?
_____	he		

✔		
Yes,	we	_____ .
	he	**does.**

✖		
No,	we	**don't.**
	he	_____ .

> AB, p. 100. Ex. 3 ▶

7 Make five true sentences. Use *(not) have to* + the phrases in the box. In pairs, compare answers. Did you learn anything new about each other?

> get up early during the week
> work / study at weekends
> drive to work / school
> learn English for my (future) job
> pay a lot of tax   use the internet a lot

1 *My mother has to get up early during the week.*

Listening

8 (4.5) Listen and write *Joe* or *Sally*.

1 _____ says men and women have the same obligations.

2 _____ says men don't think of housework as an obligation.

9 Listen again. Mark (∧) the two missing words for each line and write them in the chart. Do you agree with Joe or Sally?

		Missing words
Joe:	But wait a minute, Sally. Do∧women have to wear∧hats?	_only_ _____
	What men? Men have those hats!	____ ____
Sally:	No, I think so, Joe. Not usually. Well, some men, but not many.	____ ____
	Not the two hats … Men think different!	____ ____
Joe:	What about me? I do housework. I cook the family,	____ ____
	wash dishes …	____ ____
Sally:	Really? But you do it because you have to?	____ ____
	Do you think of housework as obligation? Or you do it	____ ____
	when you can, or when you want, or just 'help'?	____ ____
Joe:	Erm …	
Sally:	Well, Joe, that's big.	____ ____

Speaking

10 In small groups, answer the questions. Remember three interesting things to tell the class.

Are you doing your share?

Answer Sally's questions to see who does the housework in your house!

1 Who does what in your house?

2 What do you have to do?

3 What don't you have to do?

4 When you were 12, what did you have to do at home?

5 When and how did you learn to (do the ironing)?

A: *My husband usually cooks. I don't have to do it.*

B: *I don't have to do anything in my house! My mother does everything.*

C: *Lucky you! I live alone, so I have to do everything!*

4B Do you want some biscuits?

Speaking

1 (4.6) Name three fruits, three vegetables and six drinks in English. Word Bank 12, p. 75.

Reading

2 (4.7) Listen and read. Circle the ten differences you hear.

Breakfast Around the World

A Breakfast in _____ .

B Breakfast in _____ .

What do people usually have for breakfast? Well, that of course depends on where they're from.

In France, for example, people don't usually eat a lot in the morning. They have some croissants or bread, with jam or butter, and a cup of coffee or hot chocolate. The Japanese have soup (soybeans and vegetables, or fish) and eggs. In Nigeria, they also have soup, made with peppers, vegetables and meat or fish. Turkish breakfast usually includes cheese, olives, tomatoes, cucumber and bread with honey or jam. And they drink coffee, tea or yoghurt. Breakfast in North America, Australia and Britain can be very large. They often eat toast, cereal, eggs and some meat, usually bacon. The Americans also like pancakes. In Australia, they eat fruit, too, and in both countries, milk is a favourite breakfast drink.

We're all wonderfully different! But one thing the world has in common – we all get hungry for breakfast!

3 Look at the photos. Complete A and B in the text with the countries. Did any breakfast information surprise you?

4 In groups, compare breakfast in your country with two other countries.

A *In Egypt, we (don't) usually have … .*

B *Yes, and Arab people (never) eat … .*

C *And in Japan, they (don't) drink … .*

Listening

5 (4.8) Look at the photo. Imagine who they are and what they're all saying. Listen to part of the dialogue and check. What do you think they say next?

6 (4.9) Listen and check. Which six food and drink items do they talk about? What does Cal eat?

7 In pairs, complete the dialogue. Listen again and check.

Dad: Wh_ _ d_ y_ _ wa_ _ t_ e_ _, Cal?

Cal: Noth_ _ _, Dad. I'_ n_ _ hung_ _.

Mum: Wh_ don't y_ _ finish your c_ _ _ _ _ _ ?

Cal: N_, th_ _ _ _ _. C_ _ I h_ _ _ some

_ _ _ _ _, p_ _ _ _ _ ?

Mum: Wh_ don't y_ _ h_ _ _ some _ _ _ _ _ ?

Cal: N_, th_ _ _ _ _. Ju_ _ w_ _ _ _.

Dad: OK. He_ _ y_ _ a_ _. Wo_ _ _ y_ _ l_ _ _

some b_ _ _ _ _ _ _ ?

Cal: No, I d_ _ _ w_ _ _ any b_ _ _ _ _ _ _.

Dad: D_ y_ _ w_ _ _ some t_ _ _ _ ?

Cal: Y_ _ kn_ _ I do_ _ li_ _ t_ _ _ _.

Mum: Ho_ ab_ _ _ an a_ _ _ _ ?

Cal: O_. I'll have half an a_ _ _ _ !

Grammar

8 Look at the yellow words in Exercises 2 and 7. Complete the Grammar box with *some* or *any*.

Countable / uncountable nouns and offers			
		Countable	Uncountable
➕	They have	_____ croissants.	_____ meat.
➖	I don't want	_____ eggs.	_____ cereal.
❓	Do you have	any olives?	any jam?
Offers	Would you like	_____ biscuits?	_____ cereal?
	Do you want	an apple?	_____ toast?

_____ is positive. Use it in questions when they are:

a offers

b requests

Can I have _____ more coffee, please?

AB, p. 101. Ex. 3 ▶

Speaking

9 Roleplay in pairs. B is visiting A's house for the first time.

A: Offer B food and drink from Word Bank 12. Get B to accept two items.

A: *Would you like a coffee / some biscuits? How about ...?*

B: Listen and answer A. Make excuses, for example, using the phrases in the Tip box.

B: *Yes, please. / No, thanks. I'm not very hungry.*

Begin like this:

A: (Opening front door) *Hello (B). How are you? Please come in.*

> **Tip**
>
> **Making excuses**
>
> I'm | (not very) hungry / thirsty.
> | on a diet.
> | allergic to (orange juice).
>
> I had one / some for lunch.
> Thanks, but I'm full. I had a big breakfast.

Tonight? Sure! I'd love to!

The gondola ride

Theatre information
Majestic Theatre
New York

Current show
The Phantom of the Opera

Opened
January 26, 1988

Performances
Mon–Sat at 8 p.m.
Wed & Sat at 2 p.m.

Running time
2 hours 30 minutes

Tickets
$20–$80

Don't miss the American production of *The Phantom of the Opera*, the fantastic musical by Britain's Andrew Lloyd Webber, an enormous success in the USA since 1988.

The music is gorgeous (*All I Ask of You*, *Music of the Night*), and the special effects are fabulous. Enjoy the scary gondola ride under the Paris Opera House and the famous chandelier scene. And of course there's the brilliant performance of the actors. An unforgettable theatrical experience! A great night out for all the family!

For more information go to
http://www.thephantomoftheopera.com

Discount tickets!

Go to TKTS in Times Square (between Broadway and 47th Street). They offer 25% and 50% discount tickets for same-day shows.

Reading

1 In one minute, read the review and circle the answers to these questions. Check in pairs.

1 Who wrote *The Phantom of the Opera*?

2 Where does the gondola go?

3 What time does it start on Thursdays?

4 How many performances are there in the afternoon?

5 How long is the musical?

6 Where can you get cheap tickets?

2 Read the review again and find:

1 the names of two songs

2 seven positive opinion adjectives

3 the best five things in *The Phantom*.

Would you like to see this production?

Listening

3 (4.10) Listen and tick (✓) the five correct answers.

1 The two people in the photo are:

Chloe and Joe ☐

Zoe and Jay ☐

2 He invites her to:

sit down ☐

have lunch ☐

have a drink ☐

watch a DVD ☐   go to the theatre ☐

4 Put the dialogue in order, 1–14. Listen again, check and repeat.

13	We could go next week, then …
___	Sure! That would be great!
___	Of course. Listen, Zoe. Would you like to see *The Phantom of the Opera* tomorrow night?
___	Yes, I am today. I'm really hungry!
1	Hey, Zoe! What are you doing here?
8	Yes, please. I'd like some water.
___	Because I promised to look after my nephew …
___	Fine! Are you eating alone?
11	Why not?
___	Yes, I'd love to. No, wait! Sorry, I can't tomorrow.
___	Hi, Jay! How are you?
5	So please, sit down. Let's have lunch together.
___	Sure. Would you like a drink?
___	Well, OK, if you're paying!

5 Match eight lines from the dialogue with their function.

Offering: ___

Saying 'Yes', politely: _8_ and ___ and ___

Asking for a reason: ___

Saying why: ___

Inviting: ___ and ___

Saying 'No', politely: ___

Grammar

6 Complete the Grammar box using phrases from Exercise 4.

Offering	
W_ _ _ _ you _ _ _ _ something to drink?	_ _ _ _ , _ _ _ _ _ _ _ _ . / No, thanks.

Inviting			
W_ _ _ _ y_ _ l_ _ _ t_ see a play tonight? L_ _ _ have dinner together tomorrow.	+	Sure, Yes,	why, _ _ _ _? that _ _ _ _ _ _ _ be nice! _ _ _ _ _ _ to.
We _ _ _ _ _ _ go next weekend, then.	–	Sorry, _ _ _ _ _.	

Asking for a reason	
_ _ _ _ _ not?	_ _ _ _ _ _ _ _ _ I'm busy tonight.

Contractions I'd = I would

(AB, p. 102. Ex. 3 ▶)

Pronunciation

7 (4.11) Listen and copy the **intonation**.

Would you like to have lunch?

Yes, I'd love to.   Sorry, I can't.

(4.12) In pairs, listen and respond to five more invitations.

8 In pairs, ask *Do you like …?* and *Would you like to … + future time?* for each picture. Agree something to do together.

A: *Do you like playing cards?*

B: *Yes, I do, sometimes.*

A: *Would you like to play cards this weekend?*

B: *I'd love to. But I can't because I'm not here this weekend.*

9 Get a card from your teacher. Make dialogues. Choose your best version to act for the class.

I'm going to visit my brother

Pronunciation

1 (4.13) What's the first and last sound in *going*? Word Bank 8D, p. 71.

Listening

2 In pairs, use the words in the box to remember Zoe and Jay's story.

> Zoe & Jay   met   restaurant
> lunch together   invited   see *The Phantom*

3 (4.14) Listen to Zoe and Jay and circle the correct option.

1 They *liked / didn't like* the show last week.

2 Jay *invited / didn't invite* Zoe to go out again.

3 Zoe *accepted / didn't accept* the invitation.

4 She *has / doesn't have* plans for next weekend.

5 She *loves / hates* sharks.

Grammar

4 Study the Grammar box and complete Zoe's plans.

1 I__ _____ ___ visit my brother in Australia.

2 I__ only _____ ___ stay in Sydney for three days.

3 We__ _____ ___ travel to Queensland.

4 We__ _____ ___ go scuba-diving.

be going to (future plans)		
❓ What are you going to do in Australia?	❓ Are you going to see a concert?
➕ She's going to visit her brother.	✓ ✗ Yes, I am. / No, I'm not.
➖ They aren't going to stay there long.	

Use *be* + *going to* + verb for all persons.

(AB, p. 103. Ex. 3 ▶)

5 (4.15) How does Zoe pronounce *going to*? Listen and repeat.

Listening

6 (4.16) What date is it next Saturday? Word Bank 13, p. 76.

7 (4.17) Listen to Ben's friends, Mark and Sophie. What are they going to do this weekend? Do they want to see Ben? Write the names.

Mark

Sophie

1 _____'s going to go away.

2 _____'s going to stay in.

8 Listen again. Write T (true) or F (false). Correct the false ones.

1 Mark's going to go out this evening. ____

2 He's going to be with his girlfriend. ____

3 He isn't going to watch TV. ____

4 Sophie's going to go to the beach. ____

5 She's going to be alone. ____

6 Her plans depend on the weather. ____

7 She's only going to stay for one night. ____

8 They both enjoy talking to Ben. ____

Speaking

9 Practise asking the questions in this chart. Each ✻ = one missing word.

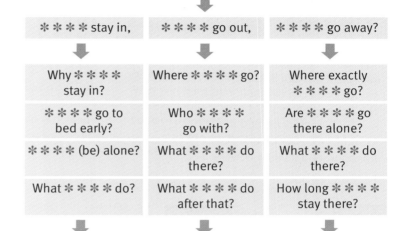

Are you going to be here next weekend?

On (Friday) night ...

✻ ✻ ✻ ✻ stay in,	✻ ✻ ✻ ✻ go out,	✻ ✻ ✻ ✻ go away?
Why ✻ ✻ ✻ ✻ stay in?	Where ✻ ✻ ✻ ✻ go?	Where exactly ✻ ✻ ✻ ✻ go?
✻ ✻ ✻ ✻ go to bed early?	Who ✻ ✻ ✻ ✻ go with?	Are ✻ ✻ ✻ ✻ go there alone?
✻ ✻ ✻ ✻ (be) alone?	What ✻ ✻ ✻ ✻ do there?	What ✻ ✻ ✻ ✻ do there?
What ✻ ✻ ✻ ✻ do?	What ✻ ✻ ✻ ✻ do after that?	How long ✻ ✻ ✻ ✻ stay there?

What ✻ ✻ ✻ ✻ have to eat and drink?

What time ✻ ✻ ✻ ✻ go to bed?

10 In pairs, ask and answer about your plans for next weekend. Any coincidences?

A: *What are you going to do on Friday evening?*

B: *(I think) I'm going to ... .*

A: *Are you going to (travel) next weekend?*

B: *Yes, I am. / No, I'm not. / Perhaps.*

> **Tip**
> Maybe. = Perhaps. = I'm not sure.
> I don't know. It depends (**on** the weather).

11 Class survey: Any **big** plans? Are you going to (...) soon? Choose a question to ask as many classmates as you can in three minutes. Tell the class any surprise answers that you find.

buy a new car   change your job

get married   emigrate

go scuba-diving

move house

retire   travel abroad

?

How do you get around?

Reading

1 Read in groups. A: read about Laura; B: read about Kim Jung; C: read about Deniz. Tell each other what you remember.

I travel to the university every day. The journey usually takes about 45 minutes by car. But by public transport, I have to walk to the bus stop and then take the bus into the town centre. Then I have to wait for the train, which is often late! The train journey takes half an hour and then I have to walk for 15 minutes from the station to the university. The journey takes two hours! Sometimes they cancel the train and then I miss my lectures. You can't depend on public transport and it takes ages to get anywhere!

Laura, Liverpool

I commute by bike. The journey is five kilometres and it takes me about 15 minutes. It's a really good way to start the day! I arrive at work relaxed. And on the way I pass most of my friends who drive to work! I'm in the fresh air, it doesn't cost anything and I'm getting lots of exercise. Perfect!

Kim Jung, Seoul

I started driving to work ten years ago, and the journey took me half an hour. Now it takes me an hour or more. There are lots of traffic jams and lots of cars on the roads now – it's terrible. I often have to sit in a jam for ten minutes just listening to the radio and getting angry! When I get to work, I'm often stressed and tired! My problem is that I have to carry a lot of things to work and that's impossible by public transport or on a bike. So I have no choice.

Deniz, Izmir

2 Read all the texts. Who

1 can't use public transport? Deniz and _____

2 gets to work before their friends? _____

3 would like to use a different form of transport?

_____ _____

4 has problems with traffic? _____

5 can't always do what he / she wants because of transport? _____

6 takes over an hour to get to work? _____

3 In pairs, ask and answer. Find three differences between you / your countries.

1 How do you usually get around? Why?

2 How often do you (travel by bike)?

3 When was the last time you (travelled by plane)?

4 Is public transport good / cheap in your country?

5 How do commuters usually get to work in your country? Do they commute from very far away?

> fast   cheap   crowded
> comfortable   healthy   hot
> dangerous   boring   busy   slow

Listening

4 (4.18) Listen to Zoe and her brother Charlie. What three things are making her feel scared?

5 Listen again and circle what Charlie says.

1 How is Zoe going to get to Charlie's house from the airport?

Charlie: You *get / take* the train *out of town / to the city centre*. Then get a *bus / taxi* to my place.

2 How long does it take?

Charlie: It only *is / takes* about *10 / 18* minutes.

3 How far is it?

Charlie: It's *exactly / about* two *kilometres / miles*.

Tip
1 mile = 1.6 kilometres.

Grammar

6 Study Exercise 5 and complete the Grammar box.

Getting about	
?	**+**
_____ do you _____ _____ your house (from the airport)?	I / You go _____ bus. Take a taxi / bus / train.
_____ long does it _____ (you)?	It _____ (me) about half an hour.
_____ far _____ _____?	_____ about five miles.

> AB, p. 104. Ex. 2 ▶

7 In pairs, compare your typical journeys. Ask *How ... ?*, *How long ... ?* and *How far ... ?*. Find three things you have in common.

To	From
school / university / work	your house / flat
the cinema	
your best friend's house	
the supermarket	your school / work
the airport	
the shopping centre	
the bus station	
the bank	

A: *How do you usually get to the supermarket from your house?*

B: *By car. / I drive.*

A: *How long does it take?*

B: *About 10 to 15 minutes. It depends on the traffic.*

A: *And how far is it?*

B: *It's not far. About two kilometres.*

Speaking

8 (4.19) What exactly are you going to do after class? Word Bank 6B, p. 69.

9 Find someone in the class who's going to do these things after class. Ask more questions, too.

Find someone who is going to ...	Name	Details
use public transport.	_____	_____
go home on foot.	_____	_____
go under a bridge on the way home.	_____	_____
turn left four times on the way home.	_____	_____
go past a park and a petrol station.	_____	_____
travel for over half an hour.	_____	_____

A: *Are you going to use public transport today?*

B: *Yes, I am. I'm going to take a bus and then get a train.*

A: *How long is it going to take?*

10 Imagine you've got a free ticket to fly around the world in 80 days! You can stop in only three countries.

In pairs, plan ...
- where you are going to stop
- how long you are going to spend in each country
- what you're going to do in each one
- how you're going to travel around each country.

BOARDING PASS

LUCKY WINNER!

FROM _____
3 STOPS!!!
TO _____,
_____
AND _____

VALID - 3 MONTHS

	1	2	3
Where?			
How long?			
What/ do?			
How/ travel?			

4f   The perfect holiday

Reading

1 Match the photos and the four seasons. Which is your favourite season? Why?

the spring   the summer   the autumn   the winter

2 In pairs, answer the questions.

  1 What's a podcast?

  2 Do you listen to podcasts? How often? What are they usually about?

  3 Do you ever create your own podcasts? If not, would you like to? Why / Why not?

3 (4.20) Read Zoe's blog and circle the correct prepositions, 1–9. Then listen and check.

  1 On / In

  2 in / of

  3 to / with

  4 for / down

  5 for / to

  6 of / up

  7 to / at

  8 under / around

  9 at / to

Travel podcasts to help you plan your holiday

by Zoe

(1)__ the Net, you can learn about any country (2)__ the world. You can also communicate (3)__ other travellers. This year, I downloaded a podcast (4)__ my winter trip (5)__ Sydney. It was great, and the stories were really funny, too! It helped me to decide the type (6)__ holiday, when to go (which season), which hotel (7)__ stay at and the best company to book with, how to get (8)__ , and which attractions to go (9)__ . Now I'm going to start uploading podcasts and you can soon hear my voice! And if you have a podcast to promote, please contact me. I can advertise it here, too. Absolutely free!

What's a podcast?

Basically, anybody can create an audio file on a computer. Download this onto your MP3 player and then you can listen to it on your travels.

4 Read the blog again and answer the questions.

  1 Find six ways that podcasts can help you plan your trip.

  2 Do you have to pay to advertise podcasts on Zoe's site?

  3 What four things do you need to create and use podcasts?

Listening

5 (4.21) Listen to Zoe's first podcast. Write T (true) or F (false). Correct the false ones.

1 Zoe's going to travel to Thailand. ____
2 Jay's going to stay for two weeks. ____
3 He's going to fly direct. ____
4 He bought his flight at cheapflights.com. ____

5 He's going to visit Phuket. ____
6 He's going to get tuk-tuks and rent a motorbike. ____
7 He found his hotel room at asiarooms.org. ____
8 Zoe really wants to go with him. ____

Grammar

6 (4.22) Complete Zoe's questions in the Grammar box. Circle the correct option in the rule. Listen and check. Is your language similar?

Prepositions in questions

Where are you going to travel _____?
How are you going to get a_____?
Who are you going to go _____?

Rule

In English, prepositions go at the *start / end* of questions.

Speaking

7 In pairs, plan your perfect holiday. Prepare your answers to these questions.

1 Where / travel to?
2 Who / go with?
3 How / get there?
4 What time of year / be there?

5 What / do when you arrive?
6 How / get around?
7 Where / stay?
8 How long / stay there?

Swap pairs. Ask and answer about each other's plans. Which holiday do you prefer?

A: *Where are you going to travel to?*

8 Where did you go for your first big holiday without your family? What season was it? In small groups, ask and say as much as you can. Remember a good story to tell the class.

A: *When was the first time you went away without your family?*

B: *When I was about 16 years old.*

C: *Where did you go to?*

Go to **Phrasebook 4** p. 78 ▶   Go to **Essential Grammar 4** p. 118 ▶

4A 1 Make questions. Interview your partner.

How often / do / does

you
your flatmate
your brother
your sister
your friend
etc.

cook ...
do ...
hoover ...
tidy up ...
water ...
take ... for a walk

?

A: *How often do you tidy up the flat?*

B: *Never! I hate it. My flatmate always does it!*

2 In groups of three, answer the questions. What do you have in common?

> **Obligations, obligations!**
>
> How are or were your obligations different
>
> **1** during the week and at weekends?
>
> **2** in the mornings and the evenings?
>
> **3** at primary school compared to now, at this school, where you learn English?

A: *At weekends, I don't have to get up early.*

B: *I'm very different. I have to get up early every day because I've got young children.*

C: *Me, too. When I was at primary school, I had to go to bed at eight o'clock.*

4B 3 Play FOOD & DRINK RACE. In teams, think of food beginning with these letters. Decide if it's countable or uncountable.

a b c e f h j m o p r s t w y

A: *Apple.*

B: *Yes, and an apple is countable. OK, what about b ....*

4 (4.23) Complete the dialogue with *a, an, the, some* or *any*. Listen and check.

A: Good morning.

B: Good morning. And what can I get you for breakfast, sir?

A: Well, I'd like (1) _____ cup of coffee and (2) _____ brown toast.

B: I'm afraid we haven't got (3) _____ brown toast. How about (4) _____ white toast?

A: OK. That's fine.

B: Would you like (5) _____ cereal?

A: No, thanks. But I'd like (6) _____ orange juice.

B: We haven't got (7) _____ orange juice, but we have got (8) _____ tomato juice.

A: No, thanks. Just (9) _____ bottle of mineral water, please.

B: Would you like (10) _____ eggs or bacon?

A: Yes, please. I'd like (11) _____ egg and (12) _____ bacon.

B: Oh, I'm sorry – I forgot. We haven't got (13) _____ eggs this morning.

A: Just the bacon, then, please.

5 Get a card from your teacher.

A: You're the customer in a restaurant.

B: You're the waiter / waitress.

> **Song: *Material girl* by Madonna**
>
> To find the words, google lyric + the name of the song.
>
> To find the video, google video + the name of the song and singer.

6 Choose the correct words. In pairs, compare answers.

1 _____ you like to come out tonight?

   a Do   **b** Would   **c** Can

2 Let's _____ lunch together.

   a eat   **b** have   **c** do

3 The waiter told us to sit _____ .

   a up   **b** down   **c** on

4 On Saturday, we _____ to the theatre.

   a visited   **b** watched   **c** went

5 We _____ a drink before the show.

   a had   **b** made   **c** did

7 Complete the dialogues.

A: Would you like to come out tonight?

B: Yes, I'd (1) _____ (2) _____ .

A: Let's go to the cinema later.

B: Yes, that (3) _____ (4) _____ (5) _____ .

C: Would you like to come out this evening?

D: I'm sorry, I'm busy this evening.

C: That's OK. We (6) _____ (7) _____ (8) _____
(9) _____ , then.

D: Sorry, I can't go out tomorrow either.

C: Why (10) _____ ?

4D **8** In pairs, write seven questions using the different colour routes.

9 In pairs, ask and answer the questions using the time expressions.

next ... (Friday, week, month, summer, year

tomorrow

in ... (three days, four weeks, a year, ten years' time)

the day after tomorrow, the week after next

A: *I'm going to travel to Dublin in two weeks.*

B: *Who are you going to go with?*

4E **10** Read the dialogue. Find and correct 10 more mistakes with articles. In pairs, compare answers.

Ed: How did you get here today?

Tom: Well, first I came out of my flat and took *the* lift to street. I walked to bus stop and took number 24 bus. We went along road for about 5 kilometres. We went under large bridge and past lot of shops. I got off bus and walked here from a bus stop. It took me about 25 minutes to get here. What about you?

Ed: I came on the foot. It took me about half hour.

11 In pairs, decide how long you think it takes to do these journeys. Complete the chart. Get a card from your teacher and check.

from	to	transport	time
Buenos Aires	Madrid	plane	
Warsaw	Frankfurt	plane	
Sydney	Perth	train	
New York	London	boat	
Oxford, England	Oxford, New Zealand	car	
	Around the world	bicycle	
	Around the world	foot	

4F **12** Write the questions to José about his holiday.

1 *Where did you go for your last holiday* ?

   We went to Thailand.

2 _____ ?

   With my girlfriend, Sally.

3 _____ ?

   By plane.

4 _____ ?

   About ten hours.

5 _____ ?

   In a little house on the beach. It was very quiet!

6 _____ ?

   For ten days. It was amazing!

7 _____ very expensive?

   No, it was quite cheap.

8 _____ you spend?

   About $3,000.

9 _____ around Thailand?

   No, we didn't.

10 _____ like to go there again?

   Yes, I'd love to.

Go to **Writing** 4 p. 63 ▶

name: Waen
location: Kuwait
e-mail: waen123@hotmail.com

Hello everybody @ PYEO!

My name's Waen. I'm Thai, 25, single and a nurse. I love my job because I enjoy helping people and it's really interesting, too.

I live in a rented flat in Kuwait with three other nurses. I'm working here to make money. I want to buy a flat in Chiang Mai and then I can get married. Workers come here from all over the world because the salaries are high.

I'm joining this online community because I need to learn English fast. I want to work for an international charity and it's essential to speak well and write well, too.

My family and girlfriend live in Chiang Mai. It's a busy city in the north of Thailand, full of history and people, but also motorbikes and cars! There are beautiful mountains and there's also a lovely river, called Ping. My favourite place is the wonderful Wat Phrathat Doi Suthep temple. It's over 600 years old. I miss it a lot!

Write soon and please correct my mistakes!

Bye for now, Waen

1 Read the advert and paragraph 1 of Waen's e-mail to find:

a the meaning of *PYEO*

b his nationality, age, marital status and job

c two reasons he likes his job

2 Read the rest of the e-mail and match Waen's actions and reasons, 1–6.

Action	Reason	
1 Waen's in Kuwait	_____ it's his home town and he misses it.	☐
2 He wants to buy a flat	_____ write to him and correct his mistakes.	☐
3 He's learning English	_____ then he can get married.	☐
4 He's joining the course	_____ his future job with an international charity.	☐
5 He writes about Chiang Mai	_____ practise online and learn from his mistakes.	☐
6 He wants other students	_____ he needs to earn a lot of money.	*1*

3 Read the first point in the Writing tip and study the yellow words in Waen's e-mail. Complete the sentences in Exercise 2 with *because*, *to* or *for*.

4 Read the second point in the Writing tip and study the blue words in the e-mail. Complete the rule. Then complete these sentences with *too* or *also*.

1 I study full time, but I'm _____ working at nights.

2 Now I'm doing this exercise and listening to an English song _____ .

3 I'm studying English so I can pass an exam, but _____ because I really enjoy it _____ .

Writing tip

because, to and *for*

1 Use *because* to give **reasons**. Compare it with *to* and *for* on page 5.
  *I'm studying here **because** the teachers are good.*

2 Use *too* and *also* to give **extra ideas** and **similarities**.
  A: *I study online and **also** go to a language school.*
  B: *Me, **too**! And I often have private classes, **too**.*

Rule: Use _____ before the verb and _____ at the end of a phrase or sentence.

5 Write a similar e-mail to introduce yourself to *PYEO*.

● Make notes for four paragraphs, like this.

● Write four paragraphs. Check them carefully and make sure you include *because*, *also* and *too*.

● Give your e-mail to a friend to check for you.

● Give it to your teacher.

1 Name? Age? Marital Status? From? Job? Why?

2 Where / live? Who with? Why?

3 Why / learning English?
  Why / want to join PYEO?

4 Where you / family live? Favourite places in your city?

1 Read Adela's biography. Write the paragraph titles in the boxes, 1–4.

After leaving school   Becoming a parent
~~Early life and family~~   School life

1	Early life and family

2	_____

3	_____

4	_____

My mother

My mum's name's Adela and she was born in Monterrey on March 16th, 1960. She was an only child. Her father was a mechanic, her mother a dancer, but they're retired now.

She started primary school in 1965 when she was five. She doesn't remember much about it now. She studied there for six years before moving to a private secondary school when she was 11.

After finishing school at 18, she got her first job. She worked in a supermarket in Texas for 11 months. After that, she went to university to study Literature. She graduated in 1982 and became a civil servant. She worked as a secretary and then then became an office manager.

She met Diego, her husband, in 1980. They got married in 1984 and had two children. I was born in 1987 and my brother Oscar arrived two years later. She's still a manager, still married and says she can't wait to be a grandmother!

Carmen Díaz

My mum   My dad

2 Read again and complete the years or events on Adela's timeline.

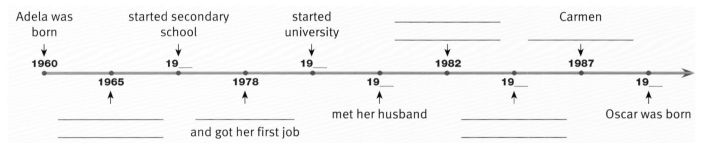

Adela was born → 1960
1965 _____
started secondary school → 19__
1978 _____ and got her first job
started university → 19__
19__ met her husband
_____ _____ → 1982
19__ _____
Carmen → 1987
19__ Oscar was born

Writing tip

before & after

Use *before / after* + verb + *–ing* without repeating the pronoun.

***After** I left university, I got married.*
***After** leaving university, I got married.*
*I had three children **before** getting divorced.*

3 Study the yellow examples in the biography and the Writing tip and correct two mistakes in each sentence.

1 Before leave school, I met my future wife and we got married two years after.

2 After get married, we have our first children – twins!

3 After we lived in a flat for five years, bought a house.

4 Complete the sentences with *in*, *at*, *to* or *for*.

1 My parents were both born _____ Córdoba _____ Argentina _____ 1944.

2 My dad studied _____ UCLA, but my mum didn't go _____ university.

3 Dad studied Medicine _____ seven years.

4 After retiring _____ the age of 65, they moved _____ Punta Del Este _____ Uruguay.

5 Write a similar timeline for one of your parents or grandparents.

6 Now write a similar biography about your person.

● Write four paragraphs. Use the four titles from Exercise 1 and your timeline.
● Include the connectors from the Writing tip.
● Check your use of prepositions.
● Give your biography to a friend to check for you.
● Finally, give it to your teacher.

My first love

1 My first love was a girl at my primary school. Her name was Amy. We were in the same class and only 11 years old!

2 We were both in the school dance team. She was always my partner. Everybody thought she was beautiful, but she only danced with me. Lucky me!

3 I can still see her face today. She had brown eyes and short black hair. She had a lovely little mouth and a small nose. She was quite tall, thin and friendly.

4 We never kissed and I didn't say anything to anybody, but I know it was love! I'm sure she never knew. We were very young and didn't understand things like that. But we danced beautifully!

5 I don't know where she is now. We went to different secondary schools and lost contact. I imagine she's married with children. Or maybe grandchildren because it was 35 years ago!

1 Read the blog entry. Write T (true) or F (false).

1 They met at school.   ___
2 Amy was short and blonde.   ___
3 They became boyfriend and girlfriend.   ___
4 They're still friends today.   ___

2 Read again and order the paragraph titles, 1–5.

[ ] Describe him or her   [1] Introduce your person   [ ] How you met and why it was special.
[ ] Your relationship then   [ ] Your relationship today

3 Read two draft blogs. Correct two mistakes with the article in each line.

	Article rules	
My first love was John Travolta in *a* film ~~the~~ *the* *Grease*. I thought	4	5
he was really a fantastic. He had the black hair, blue eyes and	___	___
a wonderful clothes. I was completely in love. I saw film 20	___	___
times and learned all songs and a dances. And I was only seven!	___	___

	Article rules	
When I was 16 and on holiday in the Spain, I met incredible boy,	___	___
Carlos. He was tall, dark, a medium build with a long, black hair,	___	___
and a green eyes. We had a two wonderful weeks together. We	___	___
stayed in contact for about year, but I never saw the Carlos again.	___	___

Writing tip

Articles
1 Don't use an article without a noun.
2 *A* = one but we don't know which one.
3 Don't use *a* / *an* with plurals.
4 *The* = we know which one or ones.
5 No *the* for names of people, films and countries.
6 No *the* for uncountable nouns.

4 Read the Writing tip. Match each correction with the correct rule, 1–6.

5 Write a similar description about your first love.

● Draft five paragraphs with the same titles as Exercise 2. Have at least a 15-minute break!
● Check each sentence carefully.
  1 Is there a noun in the sentence?
  2 Is it singular, plural or uncountable? A good dictionary tells you if nouns are countable.
  3 Does it need *a*, *an*, *the* or no article? Use the rules in the Writing tip.
● Give your description to a friend to check it for you.
● Finally, give it to your teacher.

Writing tip

1 Always write a first draft. Have a break before reading it again.
2 When you re-draft, check the articles carefully for each noun.

> **From:** akowalski@hotmail.com
> **To:** all contacts
> **Subject:** Happy New Year to all my friends
>
> Hi all!
>
> December 31st, 6.30 p.m. & we're in Rio. It's summer, hot & really exciting!
>
> Today we went shopping for champagne and flowers and we had to buy new white clothes, too. Everybody here wears white on New Year's Eve!
>
> Now we're going to meet our Brazilian friends in a restaurant near Copacabana & have a special dinner before going to the beach.
>
> At midnight, there are spectacular <u>fireworks</u> with about two million people. Wow! We open our champagne & kiss all our friends!! After that, everybody goes down to the sea. They jump over seven <u>waves</u>, <u>throw</u> their flowers in the sea and make a wish. I'm going to make a <u>resolution</u> – to stop smoking.
>
> Then we're going to dance – there are lots of bands playing on the beach. We're probably going to stay there all night & get the underground home in the morning.
>
> How about you? Hope you have a great night & … HAPPY NEW YEAR!
>
> Love
> Adam (& Jacek too)
> xxx

1 Read Adam's e-mail and number the questions 1–5 in the order he answers them.

- [ ] What's going to happen at midnight?
- [ ] What preparations did you have to make?
- [ ] Where are you going to go? Who with? Food?
- [*1*] Where are you? What season is it?
- [ ] What are you going to do after that?

2 Match the underlined words in the e-mail to the pictures 1–3 and the definition 4.

1
_____

2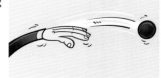
_____

3
_____

4 a promise you make to yourself on New Year's Eve
_____

3 Complete the Writing tip with words or symbols from the e-mail.

> **Writing tip**
>
> For informal e-mails:
> - start *Hello,* (1)_____ or *Hey* + the name
> - end *See you soon, Best wishes,* (2)_____ or *Lots of love*
> - use abbreviations like *and* = (3)_____ and add kisses ((4)_____) if you want to.

4 Imagine it's 6.30 p.m. on New Year's Eve in your country. Write a similar e-mail to friends about your plans.

- Draft five paragraphs to answer questions 1–5 in Exercise 1.
- Check you start and end the e-mail correctly.
- Make sure you use different connectors (see Writing tips on pages 60 and 61).
- Have a break, then re-draft, checking it again carefully.
- Give your e-mail to a friend to check for you.
- Finally, give it to your teacher.

1 (1.3) Match the colours, 1–14, and words. Listen, check and repeat.

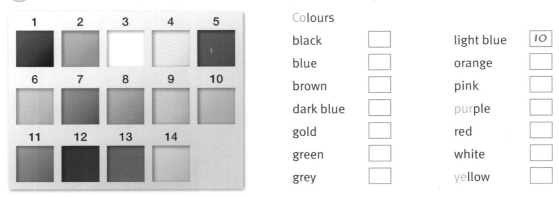

Colours

black	☐	light blue	**10**
blue	☐	orange	☐
brown	☐	pink	☐
dark blue	☐	purple	☐
gold	☐	red	☐
green	☐	white	☐
grey	☐	yellow	☐

2 In pairs, ask and answer about things in the classroom.

A: *What colour's the door?*   **B:** *It's dark brown. Are those chairs black?*

3 (1.4) Match the pictures, 1–17, and words. Listen, check and repeat.

bad	☐	expensive	☐	intelligent	**15**	old	☐
dead	☐	fast	☐	late	☐	small	☐
different (to)	☐	happy	☐	long	☐	strong	☐
difficult	☐	horrible	☐	low	☐	wonderful	☐
						wrong	☐

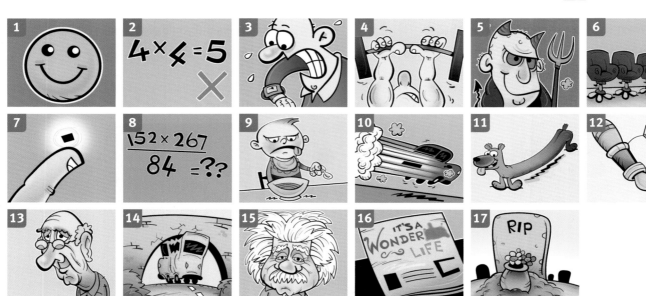

4 (1.5) Match the adjectives in Exercise 3 to their opposites. Listen, check and repeat.

alive	**17**	good	☐	short	☐	terrible	☐
big/large	☐	high	☐	similar (to)	☐	weak	☐
cheap	☐	new	☐	slow	☐		
early	☐	nice/lovely	☐	sad	☐		
easy	☐	right	☐	stupid	☐		

5 Cover the words and test your partner.

A: *What's the opposite of …?*

1 (1.9) Match the words and the pictures, 1–20. Listen, check and repeat.

☐ chat (online)	☐ feel (stressed) about	☐ give (somebody a present)	☐ sleep (well)
14 check (your e-mails)	☐ fight	☐ listen to (music, the radio)	☐ take (a photo of ...)
☐ do (exercise)	☐ fly (from ... to ...)	☐ prepare (a meal)	☐ talk (on the phone) to ...
☐ drink (a lot)	☐ go for a run	☐ see (the doctor)	☐ wait (for a bus)
☐ eat (a burger)	☐ get (a train)	☐ send (somebody a text)	☐ watch (a film on TV)

2 Cover the words and test your partner.

A: *What's he doing*   **B:** *He's doing exercise. What are they doing?*

 1B p.6

1 (1.10) Match the words and phrases, a–r, with the sentences, 1–13. Listen, check and repeat.

a   bill
b   borrow
c   broke
d   by cheque
e   by credit card
f   by debit card

g   cash
h   a cash point
i   change (n)
j   change (v)
k   a cheque book
l   discount

m   notes
n   pocket money
o   salary
p   sales
q   save
r   spend

1

I prefer paying 9 .

2

I usually pay ☐ .

3

Can I pay ☐ ?
Good. Oh, and can I ☐ a pen, please?

4

Can I have the ☐ , please?

5

My ☐ is very low.
I'm always ☐ .

6

These are hundred euro ☐ .

7

This is ☐ .

8

Here's your ☐ .

9

January ☐ . 50% ☐ on all items.

10

I get £10 ☐ a week. But I ☐ it all. I never ☐ it!

11

Look! There's ☐ ! Let's get some money.

12

Paying ☐ is very easy!

13

I'd like to ☐ 100 dollars into euros, please.

2 Cover the words and phrases, look at the pictures and test yourself. Can you remember them all?

 1C p.8

1 (1.14) Match the singular clothes and the pictures, 1–9. Listen, check and repeat the clothes with their colours.

1 *a black jacket*

Singular

a coat ☐
a dress ☐
a jacket ☑ *1*
a shirt ☐
a skirt ☐
a suit ☐
a sweater ☐
a top ☐
a T-shirt ☐

Plural

jeans ☐
shoes ☐
shorts ☐
socks ☐
tights ☐
trainers ☐
trousers ☐

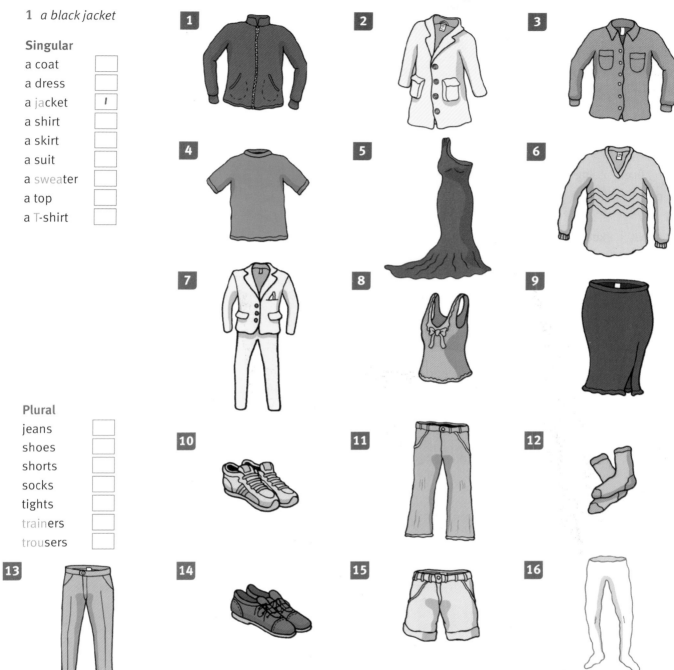

2 (1.14) Match the plural clothes and the pictures, 10–16. Listen, check and repeat.
Which two items have a different vowel sound from their colours?

3 In pairs, A cover the words. Look at the pictures and try to remember the words.
B: Look at the words and try to help A.

A: *I can't remember number 9.*

B: *The first letter is S. It has five letters. It finishes with T. The second letter is K. The middle sound is 'er'!*

A: *Oh yes, a skirt!*

 1D p.10

67

1 Match the words and the places, 1–12.

a church ☐
a hairdresser's ☐
a hospital ☐
an internet café ☐
a lake ☐
a library ☐
a newsagent's ☐
an office building ☐ 7
a police station ☐
a river ☐
a street market ☐
a swimming pool ☐

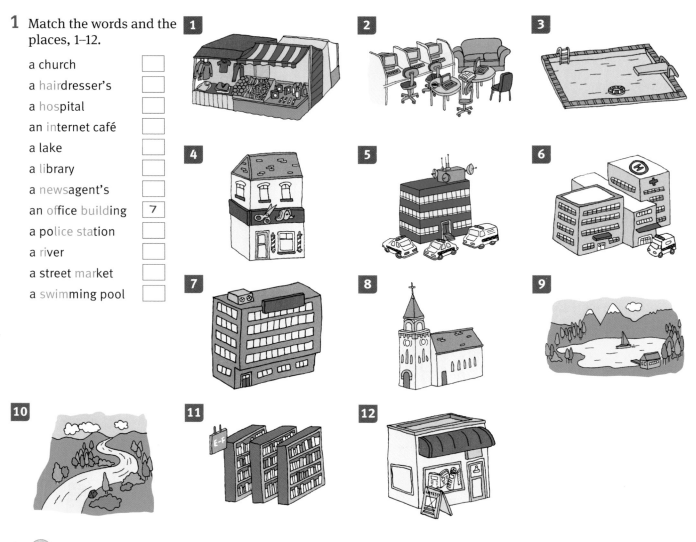

2 (1.16) Match the words and the places, 13–19. Guess the pronunciation of the 19 words. Listen and check.

a block of flats ☐
a bookshop ☐
a car park ☐
a chemist's ☐
a petrol station ☐
a shopping centre ☐
the underground ☐

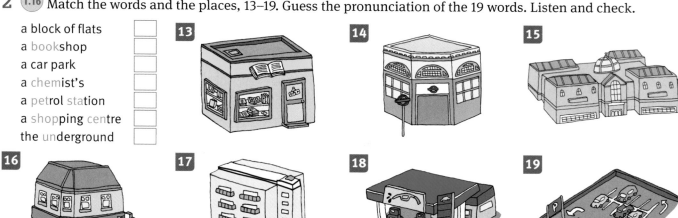

3 Cover the words and test your partner. Can you remember all 19 places on this page?

   A: *What's this in English?*   **B:** *It's a petrol station.*

 1E p.12

Prepositions

A

1 (1.22) Match the prepositions and the numbers on the picture. Listen, check and repeat.

behind ☐
between ☐
in front of ☐
inside ☐
near ☐
next to ☐
opposite ☐ *1*
outside ☐
under ☐

2 Cover the words and test your partner.
Can you both remember them all?

A: *Where's the petrol station?*

B: *Near the internet café.*

1F p.14

B

1 (4.19) Listen to and read Jacques' story. Match the prepositions and the numbers on the picture.

Jacques went from Paris to Vladivostok by train. Then he sailed around Korea. He went out of the Sea of Japan and into the Yellow Sea. After that, he sailed along the coast of China. He went under the Donghai Bridge and then sailed past Shanghai to Canton. Next, he went across China by bus. Then he climbed up Mount Everest. After that he climbed down Mount Everest. Finally, he flew over Central Asia and Europe back to Paris.

☐ across
☐ along
☐ down
1 from … to
☐ into
☐ out of
☐ over
☐ past
☐ around
☐ (back) to
☐ under
☐ up

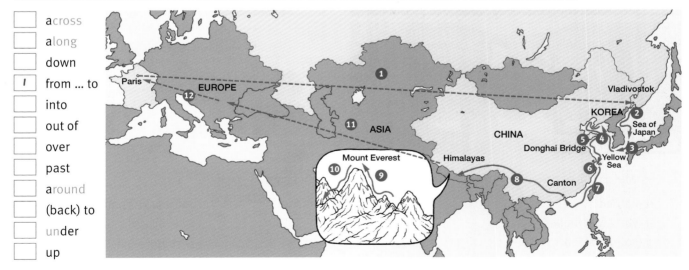

2 Cover the words and test yourself.

3 In pairs, practise the story. A: You're Jacques telling your friends your plans for the trip.
B: Listen and respond using the examples.

A: *First I'm going to go from Paris to …*

B: *Really, Jacques! Wow! Are you sure? Why? Great! You're not! Are you crazy?*

 4E p.55

A biography

1 **2.9** Match the expressions and the pictures, 1–10. Listen, check and repeat.

get married	☐	graduate from university	☐	meet (your) partner	☐
get (your) first moped	☐	have a baby	*1*	start school	☐
get (your) first job	☐	leave school	☐	be born	☐
go abroad (for the first time)	☐				

2 Cover the words and test a partner. Can you remember them all?

A: *What's she doing in Picture 1?*

B: *She's being born.*
What's she doing in ...?

2D p.24

A (2.16) Listen and repeat the sound and three words for each sound.

2F p.28

B (3.2) Listen and repeat the sound and three words for each sound. Think of another word for each sound.

3A p.33

C (3.18) Listen and repeat the sound and three words for each sound. Think of another word for each sound.

3F p.43

D (4.13) Listen and repeat the sound and three words for each sound. Can you pronounce all 24 sounds?

4D p.52

1 (3.12) Match the words and the parts of the face, 1–7. Listen, check and repeat.

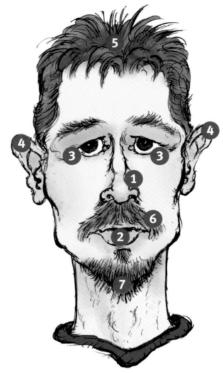

The face

a beard	7
a moustache	
a mouth	
a nose	
ears	
eyes	
hair	

Hair

bald	
blonde	
curly	
long	
short	

2 (3.12) Match the words and the hair pictures, 8–12. Listen, check and repeat.

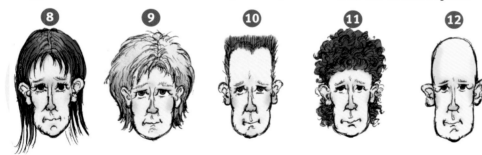

Build

fat	
short	
slim	
tall	
thin	
medium build	
medium height	

3 (3.12) Match the words and the build pictures, 13–19. Listen, check and repeat.

4 Cover the words and test yourself. Can you remember them all?

 3E p.41

1 (3.16) Cover the words in each column. In pairs, look at the pictures and say each phrase. Listen, check and repeat.

2 Test a partner. A: Say a word or phrase. B: Say the preposition.

A: *the beach*   **B:** *At the beach.*

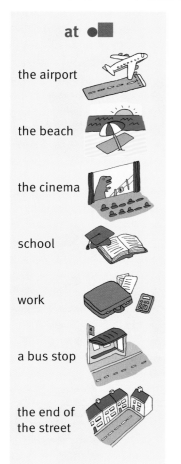

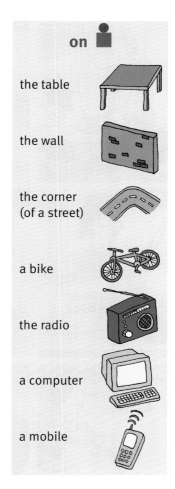

at ●■

the airport	
the beach	
the cinema	
school	
work	
a bus stop	
the end of the street	

in ◉

a city		a kitchen	
a country		a taxi	
a street		the corner (of a picture)	
the centre / the middle		a traffic jam	
a shop		the dictionary	
bed		a photo	
a park			

on 👤

the table	
the wall	
the corner (of a street)	
a bike	
the radio	
a computer	
a mobile	

Time

night	the morning / afternoon / evening	December 31st
half past seven	five minutes	New Year's Day
weekends	the 1960s	Monday
Christmas	2009	Saturday morning
the age of 60	December	

3 (3.16) Listen and repeat. Learn the nine expressions.

I'm busy at the moment.	At least we're alive.	I'm in a hurry.	We've got nothing in common!	Work in progress.
Book in advance.	The flight's on time.	Mum's on holiday.	We're here on business.	

3F p.43

1 (4.1) Match the phrases and the pictures, 1–5. Listen, check and repeat. Which three activities have the sound /ɒ/?

do housework [5]　　do the shopping [ ]　　do the washing-up [ ]

do the ironing [ ]　　do the washing [ ]

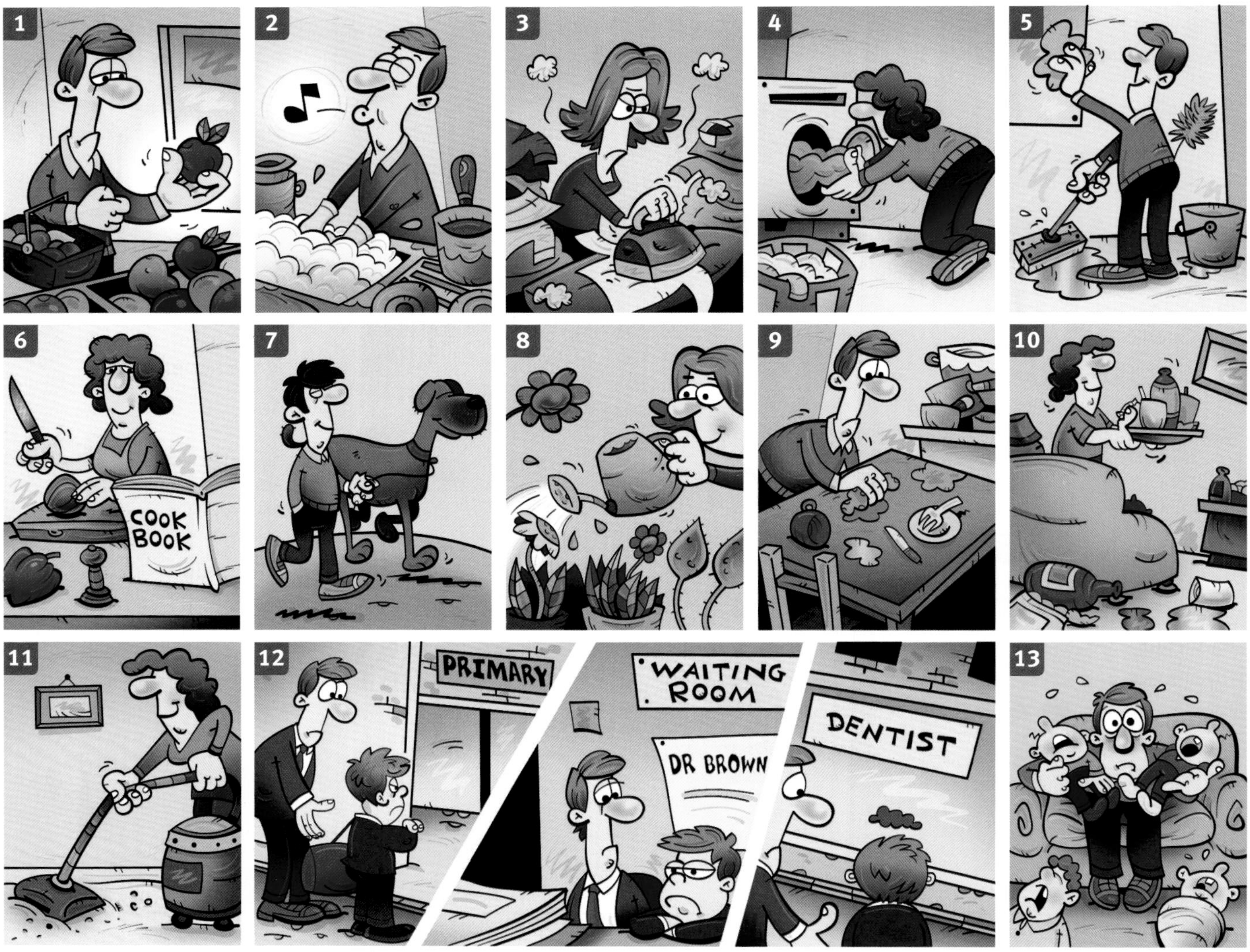

2 (4.1) Match the phrases and the pictures, 6–13. Listen, check and repeat in the past tense. Which one is irregular?

clean (the kitchen) [ ]　　take his child to school (the doctor's, the dentist's.) [ ]

hoover the floor [ ]　　take the dog for a walk [ ]

look after children [ ]　　tidy up (the living-room) [ ]

prepare a meal [ ]　　water the plants [ ]

3 Cover the words. Interview your partner from the pictures.
Ask *How often ...?*, *Do you enjoy ...?* and *Did you (...) yesterday?*

A: *How often do you cook?*

B: *Only at the weekends. Did you cook yesterday?*

A: *No, I didn't. My partner prepared a meal. It was great!*

B: *Lucky you! So how often do you cook?*

A: *Never, I hate it!*

◀ 4A p.46

1 (4.6) Match the words and the pictures, 1–24. Write *U* next to the 15 uncountable nouns.
Say *some* for the uncountable nouns or the number you can see. Listen, check and repeat.

some bread, five …

- [ ] apples
- [8] bacon U
- [ ] bananas
- [ ] beer
- [ ] biscuits
- [ ] bread
- [ ] butter
- [ ] carrots
- [ ] cereal
- [ ] cheese
- [ ] chicken
- [ ] eggs
- [ ] fish
- [ ] honey
- [ ] marmalade
- [ ] meat
- [ ] mineral water
- [ ] orange juice
- [ ] potatoes
- [ ] rice and pasta
- [ ] soft drinks
- [ ] toast and jam
- [ ] tomatoes and cucumber
- [ ] yoghurt

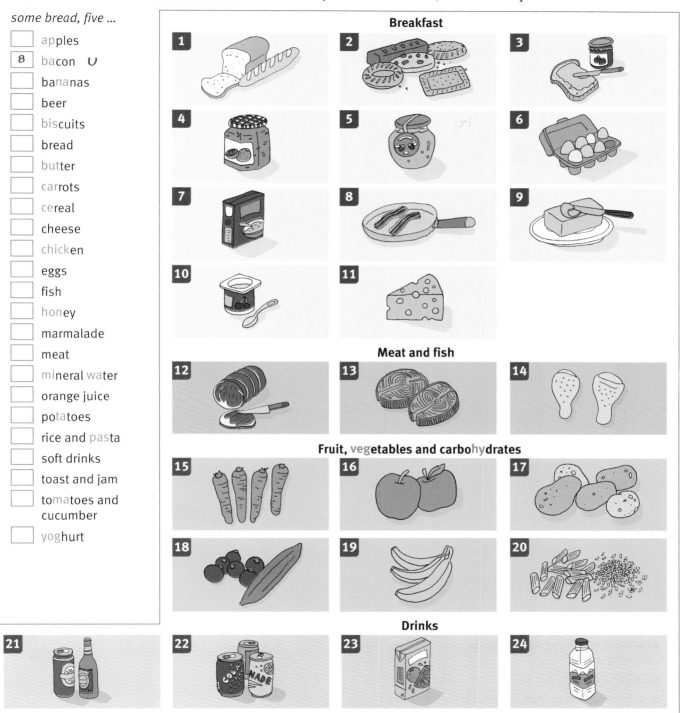

Breakfast (pictures 1–11)

Meat and fish (pictures 12–14)

Fruit, vegetables and carbohydrates (pictures 15–20)

Drinks (pictures 21–24)

2 Cover the words, point at a picture and test your partner.

3 Ask and answer about your typical breakfast, lunch and dinner.

A: *What do you usually have for breakfast?*

B: *I usually have toast and orange juice. How about you?*

A: *Nothing! I never eat in the morning.*

 4B p.48

Tip

Special plurals

The plural of some words ending in *o* = + *es*

potat**o** + s → potat**oes**
tomat**o** + s → tomat**oes**

BUT

kil**o** + s → kil**os**

1 Write the correct names of last month, this month and next month on the calendars. Write the correct initials for the days – S, M, T, W, T, F or S – too. Check the number of days is correct too.

2 Put symbols on the calendar. Mark:

- **this evening** with a ☐ (box)

- **yesterday** with a ◯ (white circle)

- **last** Tuesday with a ▲ (triangle)

- a month **ago** with a ✚ (cross)

- **the day before yesterday** with a ☹ (sad face).

- **tomorrow morning** with a ★ (star)

- **the day after tomorrow** with a ☺ (happy face).

- **next Thursday** with a ● (black circle).

- **the weekend after next** with a ✔ (tick).

- **in two weeks** with a 😮 (surprised face)

- **next month** with a ♥ (heart).

3 (4.16) Listen and repeat the six underlined phrases. How do you say them in your language?

4 Imagine today's 1st July. Test your partner.

A: *What day was yesterday / the day before yesterday / last Monday?*

B: *It was the 30th.*

A: *What day is tomorrow / the day after tomorrow / next Saturday?*

 4D p.53

Last month

		1	2	3	4	5
6	7	8	9	10	11	12
13	14	15	16	17	18	19
20	21	22	23	24	25	26
27	28	29	30			

This month

		1	2	3	4	5
6	7	8	9	10	11	12
13	14	15	16	17	18	19
20	21	22	23	24	25	26
27	28	29	30			

Next month

		1	2	3	4	5
6	7	8	9	10	11	12
13	14	15	16	17	18	19
20	21	22	23	24	25	26
27	28	29	30			

Unit 1

1 (P.1) Listen. How do you say these phrases in your language? Translate the phrases in pencil.

English	Your language
That's why …	
That's nice.	
Take your time.	
Never mind!	
I can't believe it!	
What's up?	
Are you coming?	
… at the moment.	
I'll be there in 10 minutes.	
Probably (not) …	
How are you feeling?	
We need to have fun!	
Over there.	
Can I try (it / them) on?	
Which one(s)?	
Cool!	
I'll take it / them!	
Don't forget …	
… around here …	
It's free.	
Keep the change.	
Have you got any tissues?	
Say hello from me.	

2 Cover the translations and test yourself. Can you remember the meaning in your language?

3 Cover the English. Look at your translations. Can you remember the phrases in English?

Unit 2

1 Erase the translations in Unit 1 you don't need now.

2 (P.2) Listen. Translate these phrases into your language in pencil.

English	Your language
I'm still (at school).	
In the 1990s …	
When I was a child …	
Ten years ago …	
Take me to (the airport).	
book a ticket	
check in (online)	
I'm in a hurry!	
the next flight to …	
He worked as a teacher.	
What do you think of …?	
Why not?	
especially (that song)	
I guess I'm too young!	
Did you have a good weekend?	
No, it was terrible!	
Are you crazy?	
Of course not!	
You forgot (the meeting).	
That's all.	
What's wrong (with me)?	
How about you?	

3 Listen to your CD regularly and translate the phrases in Units 1 and 2 in your mind. Can you remember them all?

Phrasebook

Unit 3

1 Erase the translations in Units 1 and 2 you don't need now.

2 (P.3) Listen. Translate these phrases into your language in pencil.

English	Your language
Can you hear me?	
Nothing serious.	
You're joking!	
No, seriously ...	
What do you mean?	
I don't think so.	
That's right.	
Take care.	
Are you ready?	
Yeah, go on.	
That's excellent news!	
None (at all)!	
At least three a day	
Come on, guys, please!	
I can type quite fast.	
again and again ...	
until you get it right ...	
English is everywhere.	
I taught myself.	
nearly / almost	
Turn right / left.	
It didn't work!	
I couldn't turn it off.	
Right now!	

3 Listen to your CD regularly and translate the phrases in Units 1, 2 and 3 in your mind. Can you remember them all?

Unit 4

1 Test yourself on Units 1, 2 and 3. Erase the translations you don't need now.

2 (P.4) Listen. Translate these phrases into your language in pencil.

English	Your language
I have no choice.	
at the same time	
Lucky you!	
Why don't you (eat) an apple?	
I'm on a diet.	
I'm allergic to (juice).	
Thanks, but I'm full.	
So, please, sit down.	
Yes, I'd love to.	
Let's have lunch together.	
Sure! That would be great!	
Where exactly?	
It depends on (the weather).	
Maybe. / Perhaps.	
I'm a bit scared.	
It's a long flight!	
I can't wait to see you again.	
I'm afraid I can't ...	
This is an emergency!	
Don't worry!	
a long time	
I came on foot.	
How far is it?	
How long does it take (you)?	
I hope you enjoy it!	
You're very kind.	

3 Listen to your CD regularly and translate the phrases in Units 1, 2, 3 and 4 in your mind. Can you remember them all?

An excellent place to learn English

Vocabulary

Word Bank 1: Adjectives p. 64
Verbs: come back, translate
Adjectives: bilingual, friendly, international, a member of … , visitors

Nouns: history, an island, nightlife
Prepositions: in the middle, between

1 (1.1) Match the questions and the answers. Listen and check.

1 And what's your date of birth?
2 Hello, what's your full name?
3 What's your mobile number?
4 What languages do you speak?
5 What's your address here in England?

a It's 25 St Margaret's Road, Oxford.
b Russian and a little English.
c It's Nikolai Petrov.
d It's 077833 6443012.
e It's the 23rd of August 1989.

2 (1.2) Why do these people want to learn English? Complete with *to* or *for*. Listen and check.

1 Cristina: 'I want *to* learn English _____ help me with my studies.'
2 Mario: '_____ my job.'
3 Eric: '_____ travel round the world.'
4 Sandra: 'I want _____ learn English _____ help me get a job.'
5 Roberto: 'I want _____ learn English _____ fun.'

3 There's one mistake in each sentence. Write the correct form.

1 Taiwan is an island in China sea.

 Taiwan is an island in the China sea.

2 Malta is the lovely place to go on holiday.

 _____

3 Do tourists come to the Britain for the weather?

 _____

4 Mexico is the very interesting place to visit.

 _____

5 Japanese is very hard language to learn.

 _____

p.5 **4** Complete the text with *a / an / the* or *0* if no article is necessary.

I live in (1)_____ Mallorca, (2)_____ Spanish island in (3)_____ Mediterranean Sea. It is one of (4)_____ Balearic islands. I like living here because (5)_____ weather is lovely all year round. We have (6)_____ international airport, (7)_____ beaches are wonderful and (8)_____ food is delicious.

5 Complete the sentences with the correct word, a–d.

1 I can't do my Maths homework. It's really _____ .
 a intelligent b difficult c strong d high
2 Do you like the green clock over there? It's not very _____ .
 a cheap b similar c expensive d different
3 I hate waiting for William. He's always _____ .
 a fast b wrong c late d short
4 Cuba is a very _____ island in the Caribbean.
 a strong b short c high d big
5 Ask Jake. He always has the _____ answer.
 a right b horrible c alive d weak

6 (1.3) Listen and complete Ewa's registration form.

Malta Intensive English School

First name: ___Ewa___ Surname: _____

Nationality: _____

Occupation: _____

Date of birth: _____

Address: _____

_____

_____

Mobile phone number: _____

Languages: _____

Interests: _____

Reasons for learning English: _____

1B What are you doing?

Vocabulary

Word Bank 2: Verbs p. 65

Verbs: have a shower, wake up, wait, wait for (a bus)

Nouns: coincidences, a gym, a machine, traffic, versions

Adverbs: probably

Expressions: I can't believe it!

1 Write the *–ing* form in the correct column.

> carry come dance drive eat get give
> have make meet put ride run sleep
> smoke stop swim take use wait write

¢ + *–ing*	+ *–ing*	double consonant + *–ing*
coming	carrying	

p.6 2 Complete with the *–ing* form of the verbs in brackets.

1 'Ssssssh! Please! I _____ for a test now!' (study)

2 'What _____ Peter _____? He's very quiet.' (do)
   'He _____ a book.' (read)

3 '_____ you _____ that dictionary?' (use)
   'No, I'm not. Do you want it?'
   'Yes, please. I _____ my English homework.' (do)

4 David _____ the news on TV. (not/watch) He _____ to a football match on the radio. (listen)

3 Look at the pictures and correct the sentences. What are these people really doing? Use the verbs in Exercise 1.

1 (doing exercise)

They aren't doing exercise. They're dancing.

2 (run in the gym)

3 (drive a car)

4 (play tennis)

4 (1.4) What are these people doing? Listen and write.

1 Tina _____ .

2 Tom and Peter _____ .

3 Sally _____ .

4 Kevin _____ .

Money: save a lot, spend a little

Vocabulary

Word Bank 3: Money p. 66

Nouns: advice, clothes, education, entertainment, food, furniture, health care, housing, space, transport

Adjectives: essential, typical

Adverbs: surprisingly

Verbs: ask for (a discount), borrow, pay, save, spend (money) on

Quantifiers: a lot of, some, not any

Expressions: borrow money from (a friend)

1 Complete the sentences with the correct word, a–d. p.9

1 A lot of people don't like paying for things with cash. They like to pay by _____ .

   a credit card **b** money **c** cash **d** change

2 A: How much _____ do you spend on food a week?

  B: Not a lot. I'm a very careful person and I only buy essential things. I don't have a very big _____ .

   a time **b** money **c** bills **d** salary

3 A: How much of your _____ do you save each month?

  B: Nothing! I'm always _____ !

   a notes **b** salary **c** broke **d** bills

4 Some shops give you a _____ if you pay in cash and not by _____ .

   a discount **b** credit card **c** money **d** salary

2 Complete the questions with the verbs.

borrow	need	save	spend	take

1 Do you often _____ money from friends?

2 How much money do you _____ on entertainment a month?

3 How much do you usually _____ from cash machines each week?

4 Do you find it easy to _____ money?

5 How much money do you _____ each month?

3 Match the answers, a–e, and the questions in Exercise 2, 1–5.

a Sometimes, if I know them well.

b Not much ... I prefer to pay by credit card.

c Not very much. About £100 a week. I live with my parents.

d No, because I love shopping!

e A lot! I often go to the cinema or to a nice restaurant.

4 Circle the correct option.

1 Tony and Maria have six children. They spend *not any / a lot of* money on food.

2 We have *some / a lot of* CDs in our house – over 2,000!

3 Jen doesn't get *any / some* pocket money, but her parents buy her everything she wants.

4 Listen, Jack. I don't have *any / some* money. Can you lend me £500?

5 I don't have *some / any* time to get money from the cash point.

5 Read the chart and complete the text with the correct name.

	Brenda	Lisa	Olivia
DVDs	✓ ✓ ✓	✓ ✓ ✓ ✓ ✓	✓ ✓ ✓ ✓ ✓
magazines	✗	✗	✓ ✓ ✓
money	✓ ✓ ✓	✓ ✓ ✓	✓ ✓ ✓ ✓ ✓
bags	✗	✓ ✓ ✓	✓ ✓ ✓
CDs	✓ ✓ ✓ ✓ ✓	✗	✗
books	✓ ✓ ✓ ✓ ✓	✓ ✓ ✓ ✓ ✓	✗

In her room, _____ has a lot of DVDs, but she doesn't have any magazines. She has some money and some bags, but she has no CDs. She has a lot of books on her desk.

6 (1.5) Use the information in Exercise 5 to complete the text about Olivia. Listen and check. Then write a paragraph about Brenda.

In her bedroom, Olivia _____

DVDs, but _____ CDs.

She _____ money and

_____ bags, but

_____ books.

1D Can I try them on?

Vocabulary

Word Bank 4: Clothes p. 67
Substitute words: (Which) one, ones
Expressions: Can I help you? How much is / are ..? Would you like to try it / them on? Can I try it / them on? It's / They're only ... I'll take it / them.

1 Find 12 clothes words in the word square. Use the word bank to help you.

v	a	v	l	d	r	e	s	s
o	s	h	i	r	t	n	k	k
w	x	q	z	y	y	m	i	t
i	s	w	e	a	t	e	r	p
l	h	w	e	a	r	w	t	v
t	o	p	m	z	a	o	b	j
s	e	v	n	y	i	o	l	a
h	s	x	r	x	n	n	u	c
i	s	h	c	w	e	v	m	k
r	o	p	o	w	r	o	t	e
t	j	e	a	n	s	o	o	t
i	s	u	t	t	s	u	i	t

2 Add vowels to complete these colours.

1 r _ d + y _ l l _ w = _ r _ n g _

2 b l _ _ + y _ l l _ w = g r _ _ n

3 w h _ t _ + b l _ c k = g r _ y

4 b r _ w n + w h _ t _ = l _ g h t b r _ w n

p.11 **3** Circle the correct option.

1 (a)_____ is a very nice sweater. How much is (b)_____ ?

  a *This / These*   **b** *it / them*

2 This black suit is OK, but I prefer the brown _____ . *one / ones*

3 Can I see _____ shirt in the window over there? *that / this*

4 How much are (a)_____orange trousers? Can I try (b)_____ on?

  a *this / these*   **b** *it / them*

5 A: How much are (a)_____ trainers over there? (b)_____ 're great!

  a *this / those*   **b** *It / They*

  B: Which (c)_____ ? The black (d)_____ or the red (e)_____ ?

  c *ones / those* **d** *one / ones* **e** *these / ones*

  A: The red (f)_____ .

  f *one / ones*

  B: They're £89.99.

4 Order the dialogue, 1–12.

Customer

- [ ] Yes, please.
- [ ] They're cool!
- [ ] The brown one.
- [ ] Yes. How much is that coat?
- [ ] Thanks. And how about those jeans?
- [ ] Can I try it on?

Assistant

- [ ] They're on sale for only £34.50.
- [ ] It's £48.
- [1] Good morning. Can I help you?
- [ ] Sure. Here you are.
- [ ] Which one?
- [ ] Would you like to try them on?

5 Write your three favourite articles of clothing.

  a red and white sweater

1 _____

2 _____

3 _____

Study tip

Be selective

1 Only write in your notebook what's useful for you now. Don't try to learn language you don't need.

2 Look at the Vocabulary boxes for lessons 1A–1D. Cross out any words you don't need to learn at the moment. Try to remember the others.

There are hundreds of restaurants

Vocabulary

Word Bank 5: Places in cities p. 68
Nouns: cathedral, compass, curry, sandwiches, sights, sightseeing
Quantifiers: only … / lots of … / hundreds of … / about …

Adverbs: especially
Expressions: There is … / There are … / Buy in advance.
Prepositions of place: opposite, next to, near
Verbs: enjoy, forget

1 Complete the sentences with *There is* or *There are*.

Looking for an Amazon Adventure? Visit Peru!

1 _____ wonderful mountains in Peru.

2 _____ 5,000 Indian villages.

3 _____ a gold museum in Lima.

4 _____ beautiful churches.

5 _____ lots of street markets in the towns.

6 _____ a fascinating history.

2 Write sentences about Toronto, a city in Canada, with *there is* and *there are*.

1 people	about 2,500,000
2 important museums	about 20
3 famous tower	1
4 big rivers	3
5 international film festival	1
6 underground stations	over 60

1 *There are about 2,500,000 people (in Toronto).*

2 _____

3 _____

4 _____

5 _____

6 _____

3 (1.6) Listen and complete the map with *the chemist's*, *the hairdresser's* and *the bookshop*.

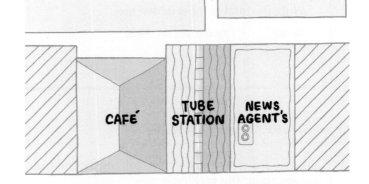

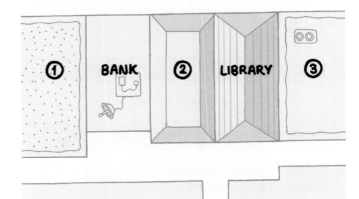

4 Look at the map in Exercise 3. Complete the sentences with *opposite*, *next to*, *near* or *between*.

1 The bank is _____ the chemist's and the bookshop.

2 The bank is _____ the café.

3 The newsagent's is _____ the tube station.

4 The library is _____ the bookshop and the hairdresser's.

5 The hairdresser's is _____ the café.

1F

Have you got a map?

Vocabulary

Word Bank 6A: Prepositions p. 69
Verbs: have got
Expressions: Is there a ... around / near here? Are there any ... in this area?

Test yourself on Unit 1

1 Do these exercises to check your progress.

2 Count your **correct** answers.
Write the total number in the box.

Total: [   ] /38 correct answers

3 Try to understand your mistakes. If necessary,
- read the **Essential Grammar**, and/or
- look at the Student Book lesson again, or
- ask your teacher.

4 How do you feel after this unit? Tick (✓) a box.

👍👍 ☐   👍 ☐   ✋ ☐   👎 ☐   👎👎 ☐

I can talk about places. (**Lesson 1F**)

1 Complete the questions with *a, an, any*. Write true answers about the area near your home.

1 Is there _____ police station?

_____

2 Are there _____ good bookshops?

_____

3 Is there _____ internet café?

_____

4 Is there _____ hotel?

_____

5 Are there _____ nightclubs?

_____

I can talk about possessions and regular actions.

2 Complete the sentences with *have got* when it's correct. If not, use *have*.

1 I often _____ lunch in the park.

2 _____ any money?
No, I _____ .

3 She usually _____ a shower before breakfast.

4 We _____ an information centre in our town.

5 They _____ two dogs and a cat.

I can use adjectives and articles. (**Lesson 1A**)

3 Put the words in the correct order. Then add *a, an* or *the* if necessary.

1 Is / Crete / the / island / Mediterranean / in / ?
Is Crete an island in the Mediterranean?

2 place / wonderful / it's / relax / to / Yes, / .

_____

3 friendly / people / beaches / are / beautiful and / are / .

_____

4 Thousands / visit / of / Crete / year / every / tourists / .

_____

5 for / weather / go / They / there / good / .

_____

I can talk about the present using the Present simple and the Present continuous. (**Lesson 1B**)

4 Choose the Present continuous or Present simple.

1 My sister _____ at home today. (work)

2 **A:** Where are you?
B: I _____ in a traffic jam? (sit)

3 **A:** What's your favourite hobby?
B: I _____ making cakes. (love)

4 He's a police officer, so he _____ at the hotel now. (not work)

5 What _____ Phil and Angie _____ ?
They're waiting for you at the gym. (do)

6 I _____ up really early in the summer. (wake)

I can talk about money. Lesson 1C

5 Read the text. Write T (true) or F (false).

Money problems? We can help …

Dear Ed

I'm 21. I live at home with my parents, but I hate it. I want to live in my own flat. I never save any money from my salary because I don't earn very much. I spend a lot of money on clothes and entertainment. I don't give my parents any money to help pay the bills, and I don't buy any food. I always use credit cards and I often borrow money from my friends, but I still can't save any money! I'm always broke. What shall I do?

Martyn

1 Martyn lives with his parents.   ____

2 He saves a lot of money from his salary.   ____

3 He only spends money on essential things.   ____

4 He gives his parents some money to help pay the bills.   ____

5 He borrows money from his friends.   ____

6 He's never got a lot of money.   ____

I can talk about clothes using pronouns. Lesson 1D

6 Choose the correct option.

1 This sweater is really nice. How much is *that / it*?

2 I need some jeans. How much are *the ones / them* in the window?

3 What a lovely coat! Can I try *the one / it* on?

4 **A:** Which shirt do you like?

   B: I prefer the *green one / green*.

5 Try these trainers on. *It's / They're* really cheap.

I can use There is / There are. Lesson 1E

7 Read about Richmond in London. Correct the false sentences.

Richmond

Church(es) ✓✓✓

Museum(s) [1]

Office building(s) ✓✓✓✓✓

Hospitals ✗

Petrol station(s) ✓✓✓

Police station(s) [1]

✓✓✓✓✓	= a lot of
✓✓✓	= some
✗	= no / not any

1 There aren't any churches in Richmond.

   False. There are some churches.

2 There are hundreds of museums.

   _____

3 There's one office building in Richmond.

   _____

4 There's one hospital.

   _____

5 There aren't any petrol stations.

   _____

6 There isn't a police station.

   _____

I can say 100 more words in English. Lessons 1A–1F

8 Cover the words and test yourself on …

1 **WB** Adjectives (p.64)

   Can you remember 14 colours?

2 **WB** Verbs (p.65)

   Can you say five things you do every day?

3 **WB** Money (p.66)

   Can you remember and spell correctly ten of the money words and phrases?

4 **WB** Clothes (p.67)

   Can you say what you're wearing today?

5 **WB** Places in cities (p.68)

   Can you say 20 places in a city?

6 **Phrasebook 1** (p.77) Look at your translations.

   Can you say the phrases in English?

2A Were you at home yesterday?

1 Complete these words with *a, e, i, o* or *u*.

1 n_ws pr_gr_mm_
2 s_ _p _p_r_
3 g_m_ sh_w
4 b_ _gr_phy
5 p_l_c _nv_st_g_t_ _n

p.19 2 Complete with *was, were, wasn't* or *weren't*.

1 Where's my wallet? It _____ here this morning!

2 **A:** _____ Albert Einstein German?

   B: Yes, he _____ from Ulm.

3 **A:** _____ you at the cinema last night?

   B: No, I _____ . I _____ at home.

4 **A:** _____ you and your sister good children?

   B: No, we _____ . We _____ terrible!

5 Don't worry! You _____ late. In fact, you were five minutes early.

6 Teka's party was great. I'm sorry you _____ there.

7 We _____ at home last night. We were at the sports club.

3 Complete the questions and answer them.

1 __Was__ George Best an Irish football player?

   Yes, he was. _____

2 _____ Oprah Winfrey an actress before she was a presenter?

   _____

3 _____ Charles Darwin American?

   _____

4 _____ Marco Polo and Vasco da Gama scientists?

   _____

5 _____ Ewan McGregor and Nicole Kidman in the film *Moulin Rouge*?

   _____

4 Correct the sentences.

1 Pelé was a volleyball player. (football player)

   He wasn't a volleyball player. He was a football player.

2 Princess Diana was from France. (Britain)

   _____

3 Karl Marx was from Russia. (Germany)

   _____

4 Luciano Pavarotti was a famous actor. (opera singer)

   _____

5 Write questions for the answers with the words in the box.

| The Beatles / American | Edith Piaf / dancer |
| the Spice Girls / from Britain | Marlon Brando / actor |

1 *Were The Beatles American?* _____

   No, they weren't. They were British.

2 _____

   No, she wasn't. She was a singer.

3 _____

   Yes, he was.

4 _____

   Yes, they were.

6 (2.1) Complete the dialogue with the correct form of *be* and *at* or *in*. Listen and check.

Sam: (1)_____ you (2)_____ home last night, Jake?

Jake: No, I (3)_____ . I (4)_____ (5)_____ the university studying.

Sam: Oh, no! We (6)_____ (7)_____ a party.

Jake: Really? Where (8)_____ the party?

Sam: (9)_____ a café near the station.

Jake: Is that right? Well, good luck in the exam tomorrow!

Sam: Exam? What exam?

Jake: Maths. Tomorrow. Nine o'clock. See you (10)_____ class!

There was no internet in the 1970s

Vocabulary

Nouns: *Countable:* a digital camera, a dishwasher, a generation, an iron, a laptop, a microwave, a mouse, an MP3 player, a personal stereo, a record, a vacuum cleaner, a video / computer game, a washing machine, a web, a window

Uncountable: air conditioning, broadband connection, instant messaging, online shopping, satellite TV, technology, the web, wireless internet

Verbs: imagine

Adjectives: automatic, commercial, digital, domestic, electric, funny

Preposition: without

Time and adverbials: (ten years) ago, in (1976), in the (1970s), when (you were a child)

1 Replace the icons with letters and find the words. Tick (✓) the things you can't live without.

1 ☐ ♣ ✳ ■ ♦ ♥ ✳ ♦ ■
   I N T E R N E T

2 ☐ ✿ ✤ ■ ♦ ▼ ▼ ♣ ■ ♦   ■ ✳
   _ _ _ _ _ _ _ _ _   _ _

3 ☐ ♨ ♣ ✿ ✤ ▲ ✤ ✿ ✤ ♦ ♥ ✿
   D _ _ H _ _ _ _ _ _ _

4 ☐ ✚ ♣ ✤ ♥ ❭ ▲ ✤ ✳ ♦ ✿
   _ _ _ _ _ _ V _ _

5 ☐ ♨ ♣ ☻ ♣ ■ ✤ ▼   ✤ ✤ ✚ ♦ ♥ ✤ ✿
   _ _ _ G _ _ _   _ _ _ _ _ _ _

6 ☐ ✳ ♣ ♨ ♦ ❭   ☻ ✤ ✚ ♦ ✿
   _ _ _ _ _ O   _ _ _ _ _

7 ☐ ❭ ✳ ▼ ♣ ✳ ♦   ✿ ✤ ❭ ❜ ❜ ♣ ✳ ☻
   _ _ _ _ _ _ _   _ _ _ P P _ _

8 ☐ ✚ ❭ ◗ ♣ ▼ ♦   ❜ ✤ ❭ ✳ ♦
   _ _ _ _ _ _ _   _ _ _ _ _

2 Make sentences using *there was / wasn't / were / weren't* and the vocabulary in Exercise 1 to talk about the 1970s.

1   *There wasn't the internet in the 1970s.*

2   _____

3   _____

4   _____

5   _____

6   _____

7   _____

8   _____

3 Complete the questions and answers.

1   *Were there any dishwashers* ten years ago?

    Dishwashers? Of course _____ !

2   _____ ?

    internet in 1950? No, _____ .

3   _____ ?

    Yes, there _____ laptops in the 1990s.

4   _____ when you were a teenager?

    Broadband? No, _____ .

5   _____ satellite TV when you were a child?

    No, _____ .

4 (2.2) Listen. Write T (true) or F (false). Correct the false sentences.

1 When Sophie was young, there weren't any colour televisions. ____

2 When Gill's grandfather was a boy, there weren't any cars. ____

3 There wasn't a phone in Rachael's house when she was a child. ____

4 When Mark's parents were teenagers, there was no internet. ____

5 When Wes was young, there weren't any public telephones. ____

Study tip

Recording words in your notebook using English only

To revise vocabulary and remember new words, you can translate them into your language. But there are other ways to do this:

- Make a note of their opposites (*beautiful / ugly; difficult / easy*).
- Write examples of expressions with that word (*sing a song, watch TV, play tennis*).
- Make word maps of word combinations:

a shower — HAVE
breakfast — HAVE — a good time

Add three phrases to the word map above for HAVE. Make your own word map for GET.

2C Sen needed to go to Beijing

1 Put the words in the correct order.

1 sir / boarding card, / Here's / your / .

_____

2 the / keep / worry, / change / Don't / .

_____

3 to / airport, / me / please / Take / the /.

_____

4 I / your / Can / see / passport, / please / ?

_____

5 delayed / to / flight / New York / The / is / .

_____

p.23 2 Complete the table with the past forms of the verbs in the box.

| arrive | check | die | hurry | live |
| marry | start | stop | study | wait |

+ –ed	y + –ied	double consonant	+ –d

3 Circle the correct option to complete the blog.

What a day!

At 8.00 a.m., I ⁽¹⁾ *stopped / waited* a taxi to take me to the airport. At 9.30, I ⁽²⁾ *hurried / arrived* at the airport. At 10.00, I ⁽³⁾ *boarded / booked* a flight. At 10.30, I ⁽⁴⁾ *booked / checked in* for the flight. Then I ⁽⁵⁾ *waited / booked* for an hour. At 11.30, I ⁽⁶⁾ *arrived / boarded* the flight.

Finally the plane arrived, and I ⁽⁷⁾ *checked in / hurried* to the meeting.

4 **2.3** Say the sentences aloud. Do we pronounce the letter *e* in the verbs? Listen and check.

1 They arriv**ed** in London in 1998. ☐ Yes ☐ No

2 We watch**ed** TV all night. ☐ Yes ☐ No

3 They play**ed** football yesterday. ☐ Yes ☐ No

4 Jim marri**ed** Susan two years ago. ☐ Yes ☐ No

5 We work**ed** 14 hours yesterday. ☐ Yes ☐ No

6 He need**ed** to fly to Paris. ☐ Yes ☐ No

7 She chang**ed** her clothes and went out. ☐ Yes ☐ No

8 They stopp**ed** at a café to have a meal. ☐ Yes ☐ No

9 He liv**ed** in a flat in the 1990s. ☐ Yes ☐ No

10 The Vietnam War end**ed** in 1973. ☐ Yes ☐ No

5 Complete the text with the past form of the verbs in the box.

| die | live | live | marry | play | play | work |

My grandfather Mario ⁽¹⁾ _lived_ in a small town in Italy. He ⁽²⁾ _____ in a chemist's. In 1967, he ⁽³⁾ _____ a girl from the same town. They ⁽⁴⁾ _____ in a house in the middle of the town.

There wasn't a cinema or a theatre. In the evenings, my grandfather ⁽⁵⁾ _____ cards with his friends in the café. He also ⁽⁶⁾ _____ football for the local football team. His wife ⁽⁷⁾ _____ when he was 55. Now he lives alone.

His life was an opera

Vocabulary

Word Bank 7: A biography p. 70

Nouns: an amateur, a primary school, a voice

Past simple irregular verbs: became, did, gave, got, had, heard, made, said, sang, saw, sold, went

1 Complete the time phrases with *at*, *in* or *on*.

1 _____ 12th October 2007
2 _____ the age of 54
3 _____ his sixties
4 _____ 2009
5 _____ July 2006
6 _____ the 1980s

2 Complete the sentences with the verbs in brackets. *p.25*

1 Pavarotti _____ (meet) Arrigo Pola when he was 19.
2 Pola _____ (become) Pavarotti's teacher.
3 Arrigo Pola _____ (give) Pavarotti free singing lessons.
4 He _____ (do) concerts all round the world.
5 He _____ (sell) millions of records.
6 Pavarotti _____ (not stop) singing when he _____ (get) ill.

3 (2.4) How do you pronounce the vowel sound in each verb? Put the verbs in the correct list. Listen and check.

> sang   had   got   go   gave
> sold   made   was   did   said
> say   sell   get   raise   sing   live

/æ/	/eɪ/	/ɒ/	/əʊ/	/ɪ/	/e/
had	gave	got	go	did	said

4 Match the verbs and the nouns.

get — school
get   a baby
go   your first job
have   your partner
leave   abroad
meet   from university
start   school
graduate   married

5 Look at the pictures and write sentences about Emilia's life. Use verbs from Exercise 4.

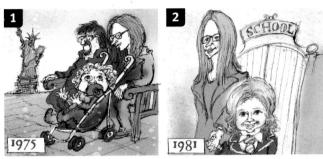

1975   1981

1997   1998

2000

2004   2007

1 Emilia was born in New York in 1975.
2 _____
3 _____
4 _____
5 _____
6 _____
7 _____

They didn't sing together

Vocabulary

Nouns: a song, a guitarist, a songwriter
Adjectives: incredible, political, musical, universal
Past simple irregular verbs: wrote

1 (2.5) What do they think? Listen and match people 1–3 and opinions a–c.

a ☐ I really love their music.

b ☐ It's all right.

c ☐ I don't like it.

p.27 2 Make Past simple negative sentences.

1 Julie bought a new CD this morning. (DVD)

She didn't buy a new CD. She bought a new DVD.

2 As a child, Mozart lived in **Germany**. (Austria)

_____

3 Victoria Beckham met her husband at a **pop concert**. (football match)

_____

4 I saw **Hulk**. (*Iron Man*)

_____

5 Charles Dickens wrote **Wuthering Heights**. (*Oliver Twist*)

_____

3 Look at Tom's room ten years ago. Write sentences about his teenage years.

_____

1 play / football

Tom didn't play football.

2 play / tennis

He played tennis.

3 listen to / music

_____

4 have / a TV

_____

5 use / a computer

_____

6 send / e-mails

_____

7 read / books

_____

4 Write about Tina's day yesterday.

1 *Tina didn't go to the supermarket yesterday.*

2 *She* _____

3 _____

4 _____

5 _____

6 _____

90

Did you have a good weekend?

Vocabulary

Word Bank 8A: Consonants p. 71

Adjectives: crazy

Verbs: cook a meal, go for a run, tidy the flat, watch TV, study for a test, stay in, go out

Past simple irregular verbs: came, forgot, left, thought

Test yourself on Unit 2

1 Do these exercises to check your progress.

2 Count your **correct** answers.
Write the total number in the box.

Total: ☐ /47 correct answers

3 Try to understand your mistakes. If necessary,
- read the **Essential Grammar**, and/or
- look at the Student Book lesson again, or
- ask your teacher.

4 How do you feel after this unit? Tick (✓) a box.

👍👍 ☐   👍 ☐   ✋ ☐   👎 ☐   👎👎 ☐

I can ask questions about the past. (Lesson 2F)

1 (2.6) Listen and tick (✓) the events Anna went to at the Glastonbury Festival.

Music

☐ Jay-Z concert

☐ New artist competition

✓ Björk

☐ Salsa lessons at El Ritmo

Poetry

☐ Open sessions

Theatre

☐ Trapeze artists Miku and Sanna

2 Write questions. Each ✱ = a missing word. Write short answers, too.

1 ✱✱ go ✱ the Jay-Z concert?

   Did she go to the Jay-Z concert? Yes, she did.

2 ✱✱ go ✱ the new artist competition?

   _____

3 ✱✱ take salsa lessons?

   _____

4 ✱✱ listen to poetry at the open sessions?

   _____

5 ✱✱ see Miku and Sanna?

   _____

I can ... talk about the past using the verb be.
(Lesson 2A)

3 Complete the dialogue with *was / wasn't* or *were / weren't*.

Libby: Hi, Joe. It's Libby.

Joe: Hi. What's up?

Libby: Where (1)_____ you last night?

Joe: Last night? I (2)_____ at home. What about you? Where (3)_____ you?

Libby: I (4)_____ at the cinema ... waiting for you!

Joe: But I (5)_____ there ... today is Wednesday!

Libby: Umm ... yes.

Joe: And we always go to the cinema on Wednesday!

Libby: Oh, I'm sorry. You're right. See you later!

Joe: OK!

I can talk about the past using there was / there were.
(Lesson 2B)

4 Complete the dialogue with *there + was / wasn't / were / weren't*.

A: Our holiday was great. It was a lovely hotel in a beautiful town and (1)_____ a lot of fantastic restaurants.

B: (2)_____ a swimming pool?

A: Yes, (3)_____ , but (4)_____ a gym.

B: What about the internet? (5)_____ wifi?

A: No, (6)_____ no internet.

B: (7)_____ lots of tourists in the town.

I can talk about the past using regular and irregular verbs. (Lessons 2C–2D)

5 Complete Julia Roberts's biography. Use the verbs in the box.

| marry | get | finish | learn | live |
| move | divorce | have | be |

Julia Roberts

Julia Roberts (1)_____
in Atlanta when she was very
young. She (2)_____
to ride a horse when she was
a girl.

In 1985, she (3)_____
to New York when she
(4)_____ high school. In 1992, she
(5)_____ married to Lyle Lovett.

They (6)_____ in 1995. She
(7)_____ again in 2002.

She (8)_____ two children in November
2004, and in 2007 her third child (9)_____ born.

I can make negative past sentences. (Lesson 2E)

6 Joe was ill yesterday. Write sentences about what he did and didn't do.

Thursday

To do
Go to the bank ✗
Make dinner ✓
Do the washing ✗
Get plane tickets ✗
Meet Sarah at 2 p.m. ✗
Tidy the flat ✗
Go to the cinema ✓

1 *He didn't go to the bank.*_____
2 _____
3 _____
4 _____
5 _____
6 _____
7 _____

I can read and understand texts about events in the past. (Lessons 2A–2F)

7 Complete the text with the correct options.

Being an International English Teacher

My name's David Scott. I (1)_____ in Scotland in
1970, but my family (2)_____ to London when I was
young. I (3)_____ to university when I was 18 and I
(4)_____ four years later. At that time, I was broke and
I (5)_____ no money to pay all the bills. Then I got
my first job as an English teacher in Madrid in 1993.
It wasn't an easy job because (6)_____ no digital
technology in the classrooms. (7)_____ no computers
or DVD players, for example. I (8)_____ my wife
Teresa, a Spanish teacher, at that school. After we
(9)_____ – in March, 2007 – we (10)_____ Argentina and
I (11)_____ a job at the British Council. It was great to
work there! Last month, Teresa and I (12)_____ back to
England. We loved living in Argentina, but we missed
our families. It was time to come home!

1	**a** were born	**b** was born	**c** born
2	**a** lived	**b** stayed	**c** moved
3	**a** went	**b** studied	**c** started
4	**a** formed	**b** graduated	**c** continued
5	**a** didn't need	**b** had	**c** didn't have
6	**a** there was	**b** there wasn't	**c** there were
7	**a** There were	**b** There weren't	**c** Were there
8	**a** meet	**b** know	**c** met
9	**a** got married	**b** marry	**c** got marry
10	**a** stayed in	**b** worked in	**c** moved to
11	**a** finished	**b** worked	**c** started
12	**a** stayed	**b** didn't stay	**c** came

I can say 50 more words in English. (Lessons 1A–1F)

8 Cover the words and test yourself on ...

1 **WB** A biography (p. 70)
   Can you remember eight verbs for talking about biographies?

2 **WB** Consonants (p. 71)
   Can you pronounce the six consonant sounds and example words?

3 **WB** Irregular verbs (p. 25)
   Can you remember ten irregular verbs?

4 (Phrasebook 2) (p.77) Look at your translations.
   Can you say the phrases in English?

Images

Vocabulary

Word Bank 8B: Consonants p. 71

Nouns: blogger, hotdog, photographer, platform

Verbs: print out, share, take photos

1 (3.1) Listen and tick (✓) the picture described.

1

2

3

2 Complete the text with the correct plural form of a noun from the box. Listen again and check.

person	man	woman	child

Natalie: I can see some (1)_____ playing football. There are lots of (2)_____ watching ... Well, perhaps about 10 ... . And there's a dog eating an ice cream. And there are some (3)_____ having a picnic. Hold on ... there's a girl riding a bicycle. There are ...

Jen: And are there two young (4)_____ sleeping on the grass?

p.33 3 Look at the photo on page 32 again and complete the sentences.

1 *There are* a lot of families _____ in a park. (relax)

2 _____ some people _____ on the grass and talking. (sit)

3 _____ a young man _____ the guitar. (play)

4 _____ lots of people _____ on the grass. (lie)

5 _____ three people _____ a picnic. (have)

6 _____ a man _____ by a tree. (stand)

4 (3.2) Complete the dialogue with *there was / there were* and the correct form of the verb in brackets. Listen and check.

Officer: And what did you see, Mr Lewis?

Mr Lewis: Well, (1)_____ a man _____ (wait) in the car park. He had a mobile phone.

Officer: And what time was this?

Mr Lewis: About half past 11. (2)_____ two young men _____ (stand) next to a red car.

Officer: And what did the man do?

Mr Lewis: He spoke to one of the men, then took his wallet and ran away!

Officer: Were there any other people in the car park?

Mr Lewis: Yes, (3)_____ two women _____ (carry) their shopping to their cars, and (4)_____ an old man _____ (sit) in his car.

Officer: Anything else?

Mr Lewis: I don't remember.

Officer: OK, thank you. That's all for now.

How much exercise do you do?

Vocabulary

Nouns: advice, a body, bottle(s), cancer, chocolate, cigarette(s), cup(s), depression, glass(es), heart attack, a mind, packet(s)

Adjectives: healthy, stressed **Verbs:** eat, cause, sleep, stress

Wh– words: how many, how much **Pronouns:** none, some

Expressions: fight stress (three) (cups) a day, a month, a week

1 What can you see in the photos?

1 *a glass of water* 2 _____

3 _____ 4 _____

5 _____ 6 _____

2 (3.3) Listen and write *E* (Emma) or *O* (Oliver) next to the photos in Exercise 1.

3 Listen again. Write T (true) or F (false).

1 Emma usually drinks orange juice, water and alcohol. ____

2 She does a lot of exercise and sometimes eats chocolate. ____

3 Oliver drinks alcohol and smokes. ____

4 He doesn't like coffee. ____

4 Listen again and answer the questions.

1 How many glasses of water does Emma drink every day?

_____

2 How many cigarettes does she smoke?

_____

3 How much water does Oliver drink?

_____

4 How much TV does he watch?

_____

5 How many hours' sleep does Oliver have?

_____

p.35 **5** Complete the questions with *How many* or *How much* and circle the correct option.

1 **Leo:** _____ wine do you drink, Tim?

 Tim: *A lot. / None. / One glass.* I don't drink alcohol.

2 **Tim:** _____ cigarettes do you smoke a day?

 Vicki: Not a lot. *None. / One pack. / About three cigarettes.*

3 **Kate:** _____ books does your son read at school?

 Vicki: Not a lot. *Just two / About 10 / None* books a month.

4 **Leo:** _____ exercise do you do a week, Ben?

 Tim: A lot! I exercise at least four times a *week / month / day.*

5 **Ana:** _____ cups of coffee do you drink a day, Vicki?

 Vicki: A lot! I think about *ten / none / one* cups, but only at work.

6 Put the words in the correct order to make questions. Add *How much … ?* or *How many … ?*.

1 you / orange juice / a week / do / drink / ?

 How much orange juice do you drink a week?

2 you / do / cousins / have / ?

_____

3 day / do / a / of / you / glasses / drink / water / ?

_____

4 exercise / do / a week / you / do / ?

_____

5 do / cigarettes / smoke / you / ?

_____

6 you / tea / drink / do / ?

_____

I can do a lot on a computer!

Vocabulary

Nouns: an application, a CV, an interview, a messenger, a photolog, a PowerPoint presentation, a scanner, skills, software, a spreadsheet, a video file

Verbs: can / can't (for ability), create, download, install, prepare, type, upload

1 Complete the phrases with the correct noun(s).

> an e-mail   a scanner   a phone conversation
> a spreadsheet   music and videos
> a video   software

1 create _____

2 install _____

3 have _____

4 upload _____

5 send _____

6 use _____

7 download _____

2 Put the words in the correct order to make questions.

1 a / you / prepare / Can / PowerPoint presentation / ?
_____

2 friend / a digital camera / your / best / use / Can / ?
_____

3 Can / web / search / you / on / information / for / the / ?
_____

4 well / speak / Can / you / English / ?
_____

5 Can / your / language / teacher / speak / your / ?
_____

3 Complete the pictures with *can / can't* and a verb.

1 Oh, no! She _can't swim_ .

2 My new secretary _____ very fast.

3 Pedro _____ English. He doesn't understand a word!

4 **Sandra:** _____ the piano?

Max: Yes, I _____ . My mother says I'm fantastic!

5 Tom _____ .

6 My wife _____ .

4 (3.4) Listen. Number the questions in the order you hear them.

a ☐ Can you cook?

b ☐ Can you speak any other languages?

c ☐ Can you use a computer?

d ☐ So can you use a messenger?

e ☐ When can you start?

f ☐ Can you help?

g ☐ Can you drive?

h ☐ And can you have a phone conversation on the internet?

I need to learn quickly

Nouns: a goal, progress, a tip   **Adjectives:** afraid, easy, exact, fast, quick, real, regular
Adverbs: carefully easily, exactly, fast, quickly, really, regularly, well
Expressions: By + –*ing* form (By practising)

1 (3.5) Listen and tick (✓) the things Louise can do well. Cross (✗) what she can't do very well.

sing ☐

play the piano ☐

speak French ☐

speak Spanish ☐

cook ☐

2 Complete the sentences with the words in the box. Listen again and check.

> badly   carefully   easily   quickly
> slowly   well

1 I saw a really interesting website about how to learn languages _____ .

2 I sang really _____ , but I wanted to learn. But it was no good.

3 I play the piano very _____ because I practise a lot.

4 I can't understand very much, so people need to speak _____ to me

5 I can understand French _____ , and I can speak quite well.

6 I like learning new recipes and I always follow them very _____ .

p.39 3 Circle the correct option.

1 She's a very *clever / cleverly* person. She learns everything very *quick / quickly*.

2 Playing the piano is difficult. You need to practise *regularly / regular*.

3 I'm very *careful / carefully* when I'm driving. You can *easily / easy* have an accident.

4 My mother can speak *good / well* German, but she speaks English really *badly / bad*.

5 What *exact / exactly* do you want to do when you leave school?

4 Complete the text using the adjective or adverb form of the words in the box.

> good   happy   healthy   regular   slow

How to live without stress

Why are other people relaxed when you feel tired and stressed? Follow our tips and learn the secret of a life without stress.

1 Make sure you exercise _____ .

2 Always sleep _____ .

3 Try to eat _____ food.

4 It's important to enjoy your food and eat _____ .

5 Finally, be _____ , and enjoy the moment!

5 Match the questions and the answers.

1 How did you learn English?

2 How did you become good at cooking?

3 How do you do well in exams?

4 How do you relax at the weekends?

5 How do you stay healthy?

a ☐ By going to classes after work.

b ☐ I study hard.

c ☐ By watching cooking programmes on TV.

d ☐ By doing lots of exercise.

e ☐ I paint and read.

The usual suspects

Vocabulary

Word Bank 9: Describing people p. 72

Nouns: a poster

Adjectives: bald, blond(e), fat, medium build, medium height, old, overweight, short, slim, tall, thin, young

1 Read and answer. What part of the face is it?

1 We have two of them on our face. We use them to see. They can be blue, green, grey, black or brown. Sometimes people need glasses for them to work well. _____

2 It's in the middle of your face, under your eyes. Your mouth is under it. _____

3 Some men have one under their mouths. They can be short or long and are usually the same colour as their hair. _____

4 Some men have one under their noses.

_____

2 Look at the people in the picture and write their name next to their description.

1 _____ is not very tall and has short, brown hair and green eyes.

2 _____ is tall and thin with short, brown hair, brown eyes and a moustache.

3 _____ is thin with short, brown hair and a beard.

4 _____ is fat with grey hair and blue eyes.

5 _____ is slim with long, dark hair and brown eyes.

 3 Make sentences. Add the verbs *have* or *be* where necessary.

1 Rafael Nadal / tall / and / he / long / dark brown / hair.

_____

2 Lindsay Lohan / very tall / and / she / long / red / hair.

_____

3 Tiger Woods / medium build / and / he / short / dark / hair.

_____

4 Katie Holmes / quite / tall / and / she / beautiful / blue eyes.

_____

5 Cristiano Ronaldo / tall / and / slim / and / he / short / brown / hair.

_____

4 Write a description of these people.

Brad Pitt
Age: 40s
Height: 1.80m
Hair colour: brown
Eye colour: brown

1 *Brad Pitt is in his forties and is medium height. He's got short, brown hair and brown eyes.*

Jack Nicholson
Age: 70s
Height: 1.77m
Hair colour: grey
Eye colour: brown

2 _____

_____

Maria Sharapova
Age: 20s
Height: 1.88m
Hair colour: blonde
Eye colour: green

3 _____

_____

3F Staying at the hotel?

Vocabulary

Word Bank 8C: Consonants p. 71

Word Bank 10: *at, in, on* p. 73

Nouns: a complaint, heating, a kettle, a lift / an elevator
Verbs: accept, complain, get angry, lie, overbook, turn left / right, turn off
Adjectives: available, noisy
Prepositions: in the corner, on the left / right, on the (sixth) floor
Expressions: by mistake   Right now!   See you in a minute.

Test yourself on Unit 3

1. Do these exercises to check your progress.

2. Count your **correct** answers.
   Write the total number in the box.

   Total: [ ] /43 correct answers

3. Try to understand your mistakes. If necessary,
   - read the **Essential Grammar**, and/or
   - look at the Student Book lesson again, or
   - ask your teacher.

4. How do you feel after this unit? Tick (✓) a box.

   👍👍 □   👍 □   👊 □   👎 □   👎👎 □

I can say where things are using prepositions.
(Lesson 3F)

1 (3.6) Complete the sentences with the prepositions
in the box. Listen and check.

| on | in | at | to | out of |

1 We're _____ room 104.

2 Take the lift _____ the 93rd floor.

3 Go _____ the lift and turn left.

4 The door to room 104 is _____ the end _____ the
   left.

5 The table is _____ the corner.

6 See you in the Empire State building _____ the
   93rd floor.

I can describe a scene using there is / there are *and
the* –ing *form.* (Lesson 3A)

2 Find and write the five differences in the pictures.

1

2

1 In picture 1, there are three children playing with
   a ball. In picture 2, there are two children playing
   with a ball.

2 _____
   _____

3 _____
   _____

4 _____
   _____

5 _____
   _____

6 _____
   _____

I can ask about quantities using How much / How many. (Lesson 3B)

3 Write questions with *How much / How many*. Answer the questions.

1 ✽✽ packets ✽ cigarettes ✽ you smoke ✽ day

How many packets of cigarettes do you smoke a day?

None.

2 ✽✽ time ✽ you spend online every week

3 ✽✽ English ✽ your teacher speak in class

4 ✽✽ coffee ✽ your friend drink ✽ day

5 ✽✽ money ✽ your family spend ✽ food ✽ week

6 ✽✽ magazines ✽ you read ✽ month

I can talk about abilities using can. (Lesson 3C)

4 Match the verbs and the nouns to make phrases.

1 use — a foreign language
2 create a video
3 cook a spreadsheet
4 upload an e-mail
5 speak a scanner
6 send tennis
7 play a meal

5 Use six phrases from Exercise 4 to write three sentences about what you can or can't do. Use *and* or *but*.

1 *I can use a scanner, but I can't play tennis.*

2
3
4

I can talk about how we do things. (Lesson 3D)

6 (3.7) Listen. Write sentences to describe what you hear. Use a verb from Box A and an adverb from Box B.

> **A** sing   play the piano   speak French   drive   ~~ride a horse~~

> **B** beautifully   ~~well~~   badly   fast   slowly

1 *This person rides a horse well.*
2
3
4
5

I can describe people. (Lesson 3E)

7 (3.8) Listen and complete the table. Then write sentences about the three people.

	Ann	Dave	Sally
tall	☐	☐	✓
medium height	☐	☐	☐
short	☐	☐	☐
thin	☐	☐	☐
black jeans	☐	☐	☐
yellow T-shirt	☐	☐	☐
brown eyes	☐	☐	☐
bald	☐	☐	☐
glasses	☐	☐	☐
black hair	☐	☐	☐
green eyes	☐	☐	☐
blue eyes	☐	☐	☐

1 Ann: *Ann is short. She's got blue eyes ...*
2 Dave:
3 Sally:

I can say 60 more words in English. (Lessons 3A–3F)

8 Cover the words and test yourself on ...

1 (WB) Computer skills (p. 36)
   Can you remember 11 computer skills?

2 (WB) Describing people (p. 72)
   Can you remember the 20 description words?

3 (WB) *at, in, on* (p. 73)
   Can you remember all the phrases with *at, in, on*?

4 (Phrasebook 3) (p.78) Look at your translations. Can you say the phrases in English?

Some women have to wear two hats

Vocabulary

Word Bank 11: Housework p.74
Adjectives: best-selling, professional
Expressions: Lucky you!

Nouns: a hat, obligations, sofa, tax
Verbs: have to

1 Match the verbs in the box and the nouns.

> do (× 3)   water   prepare   go
> hoover   travel   take (× 2)

1 _____ housework

2 _____ the ironing

3 _____ meals

4 _____ on business

5 _____ the washing-up

6 _____ children to school

7 _____ the floor

8 _____ the plants

9 _____ the dog for a walk

10 _____ to meetings

2 Which activities in Exercise 1 do you always, usually or sometimes have to do? Which ones don't you have to do? Write 10 true sentences.

1 *I don't usually have to do the housework.*

2 _____

3 _____

4 _____

5 _____

6 _____

7 _____

8 _____

9 _____

10 _____

p.47 3 Read the chart and complete the text with *have to*.

activity	Bob	Sandra & Paul
clean the house	✓	✓
do the shopping	✗	✓
look after children	✓	✓
cook for the family	✓	✓
take children to school	✓	✗
take the dog for a walk	✓	✗

Bob isn't working at the moment, so he stays at home and his wife goes out to work. He (1)_____ look after their children – Jason and Dan – and cook for them. In the afternoon, he (2)_____ take the boys to school. He also (3)_____ clean the house. He (4)_____ do the shopping because his wife does that. Every morning, he (5)_____ take the dog out for a walk, too.

Sandra and Paul are married. They have a lot to do every day. They (6)_____ do the shopping, clean the house and cook their meals. They have a young daughter, but they (7)_____ take her to school – Paul's mother does that for them. They (8)_____ take the dog out for a walk because Sandra's mother does that every afternoon.

4 Write questions about their obligations.

1 _____?

Yes, he does, and his children love the meals he prepares!

2 _____?

No, he doesn't. His wife does that.

3 _____?

Yes, he does ... every morning.

4 _____?

No, they don't. Paul's mother does that.

5 _____?

The house? Yes, they do.

6 _____?

No, Sandra's mother does that.

5 Complete the dialogue with *have to* / *has to* and the verbs in the box. What's Joe's new job?

> travel   iron   look after   do (× 3)   take

Al: Hi, Joe. How's your new job? Are you enjoying it?

Joe: It's not bad, but I'm exhausted!

Al: So, what (1)_____ ?

Joe: Well, I (2)_____ the children when they get home from school.

Al: (3)_____ you (4)_____ the washing?

Joe: No, but I (5)_____ the clothes sometimes. And I (6)_____ the shopping!

Al: (7)_____ the children to school?

Joe: Sometimes. Their parents (8)_____ on business a lot.

Do you want some biscuits?

Vocabulary

Word Bank 12: Supermarket p.75   **Nouns:** a croissant, an olive
Determiners: any, some
Expressions: How about a … ? Thanks, but I'm full. I'm allergic to (orange juice). I'm (not) very hungry. I'm on a diet.

1 Countable or uncountable? Write the nouns in the right column. Then write the plural form of the countable nouns.

uncountable nouns	countable nouns	plural
	a carrot	carrots
cheese		

2 Find and correct seven mistakes in the dialogue.

A: OK, what do we need for dinner?

B: We need a meat for Leo and Tim and some fish for Anna.

A: What about vegetables?

B: Well, we need any potatoes and a carrots. And then let's have some bananas with yoghurt and an honey.

A: OK. And we need a bread and any cheese.

B: No problem. And let's buy some bottle of wine, too.

p.49 **3** Complete the dialogues with *some / any / an* or *a*.

1 A: Would you like _____ biscuit?
  B: No, thanks, I'm on a diet. But do you have _____ apples?

2 A: Would you like _____ soft drink?
  B: Yes, please. And I'd like _____ biscuits, too.

3 A: Do you want _____ carrots with your fish?
  B: No, thanks. I don't want _____ carrots today. I'd like _____ tomatoes.

4 A: I'd like _____ pancake with _____ butter, please.
  B: OK, but have _____ honey on it, too! It's healthy.

4 4.1 Circle the correct option. Listen and check.

Customer: Can I have [1]*a / any* menu, please?
Waiter: Yes, certainly, sir.
Customer: I'd like [2]*some / an* eggs, please.
Waiter: Would you like [3]*a / some* bacon with your eggs?
Customer: No, thanks, but I'd like [4]*a / some* toast.
Waiter: Do you want [5]*some / a* jam on your toast?
Customer: No, thanks.
Waiter: How about a drink?
Customer: Can I have [6]*any / a* coffee, please?
Waiter: With [7]*any / some* milk?
Customer: Yes, please?
Waiter: Is that all?
Customer: Do you have [8]*any / a* orange juice?
Waiter: Yes, of course.

Study tip

Word cards

1 Write new words and phrases you want to learn on cards.
2 On the back, draw a picture or write a useful personal phrase or sentence or a translation.
3 Test yourself regularly.
4 Test yourself on all the cards at the end of the week.

4C Tonight? Sure! I'd love to!

Vocabulary

Nouns: a performance, a phantom, a production, a gondola, running time, special effects
Adjectives: gorgeous, theatrical   **Verbs:** promise, start
Expressions: How long … ?   I'd love to!   OK. If you're paying.   Sure, why not?
That would be great!   Would you like to … / We could (see a film).

1 Put the words in order. There's an extra word in each. Cross it out.

1 drink / you / any / like / Would / a / ?

Would you like a drink?

2 for / go / walk / let's / could / We / a / .

_____

3 I / office / has to / her / tidy / Naomi / .

_____

4 be / That / is / nice / would / !

_____

5 theatre / We / the / then / go / to / could / let's / .

_____

6 come / you / me / like / to / the / to / Would / market / ?

_____

2 Match the suggestions and replies. There is an extra reply.

1 Would you like a drink?

2 Let's go cycling.

3 Would you like to go shopping?

4 We could go for a picnic next weekend.

5 I'm hungry!

6 Let's have dinner together.

a ☐ Why don't you make a sandwich?

b ☐ Sure, why not? The weather's going to be lovely.

c ☐ Good idea. Where are the bikes?

d ☐ Yes, please. I'd love one.

e ☐ No, sorry. I'm really broke!

f ☐ Yes, that would be nice.

g ☐ No, thanks. I'm not hungry.

p.51 **3** Choose the correct option to complete the sentences.

A: (1)_____ some green tea?

 a We could have   b Would you like   c Let's have

B: Yes, (2)_____ .

 a I'd love to   b please   c thanks

A: We (3)_____ watch a DVD tonight.

 a could   b have to   c can

B: Sure, (4)_____ ?

 a why not   b I'm busy tonight   c I can

A: (5)_____ go to a party on Saturday?

 a Would you like to   b I could   c I'd love to

B: Sorry, (6)_____ . I _____ work late.

 a thanks / have to   b I can't / have to
 c I can't / 'd love to

A: (7)_____ to Istanbul, Bob.

 a Let's go   b Would you like to   c We could

B: Yes, (8)_____ !

 a I'd love to   b Let's not   c I can't

4 Follow the instructions and write the dialogues.

1 A offers a cup of coffee. B accepts.

 A: *Would you like a cup of coffee?*

 B: *Yes, please. That would be* great!

2 A invites B to have dinner. B accepts.

 A: _____
 with me today?

 B: Sure, _____ .

3 A invites B to go shopping. B accepts.

 A: Let's _____ .

 B: Yes, _____ great!

4 A invites B to have lunch. B refuses. A asks for a reason. B gives an excuse.

 A: We _____
 together tomorrow.

 B: Sorry, _____ .

 A: _____ ?

 B: _____ fly to New York
 tomorrow morning.

I'm going to visit my brother

Vocabulary

Word Bank 8D: Consonants p. 71
Word Bank 13: Time p. 76
Nouns: plans, shark, scuba-diving
Verbs: be going to, emigrate, go away, go out, go scuba-diving, have a(nother) baby, move house
Expressions: Sounds good!

1 Read Kate's diary and circle the correct option.

Tuesday 13th April

Today was a bad day! This morning, I woke up late and I arrived at work late. Yesterday (when I was early) the bus was late, but, of course, this morning it was on time!! I finally arrived at work at 9.45. My boss was very angry with me.

I'm going to stay in this evening and go to bed early because tomorrow morning I have to be at work very early for a meeting. I don't want to be late again.

Next month, I'm going to buy a car!! Then I can be early every day!

---

1 Kate woke up late on *Tuesday / Monday* morning.
2 The bus was on time on *Tuesday / Monday*.
3 The bus was late on *Tuesday / Monday*.
4 Kate's going to stay in on *Wednesday evening / Tuesday evening*.
5 She has to be at work early on *Thursday / Wednesday*.
6 She's going to buy a new car in *May / April*.

2 Correct the mistake in each sentence.

1 I'm going to start my holiday after two weeks.
2 We're going to buy a new car the next week.
3 What are you going do tomorrow evening?
4 She's going to go to university on September.
5 It's my birthday in 10th June.
6 I'm going to cycle to work Wednesday.

p.52 **3** Make questions with *going to*. Then match the answers, a–e.

1 What / you / next weekend
_____?

2 When / they / get married
_____?

3 Are / you / learn / Chinese
_____?

4 Is / Leo / do more exercise
_____?

5 they / emigrate / next year
_____?

a ☐ No, he isn't.
b ☐ They're going to get married next year.
c ☐ No, they're not.
d ☐ I'm going to see Bruce Springsteen.
e ☐ Yes, I am.

4 (4.2) Complete the dialogue with the verbs in brackets. Listen and check.

Paul: Has anyone got any plans for the weekend? Do you want to go to the cinema?

Ruby: I can't, I'm afraid. I $^{(1)}$_____ (go) to the library to study. I've got an exam on Monday.

Paul: You $^{(2)}$_____ (not study) all weekend, are you?

Ruby: Yes, I am. I have to pass this time.

Paul: What about you, Debbie?

Debbie: Sorry, I $^{(3)}$_____ (be) at my mum's until Sunday night.

Paul: Oh, dear. Nobody $^{(4)}$_____ (be) here. What about you, Jane?

Jane: No, sorry, I $^{(5)}$_____ (visit) my cousins. You $^{(6)}$_____ (have to) go to the cinema alone, Paul!

How do you get around?

Vocabulary

Word Bank 6B: Prepositions p. 69
Adjectives: comfortable, crowded, scared
Preposition: by, on
Nouns: commuters, journey, lectures
Verbs: cancel, climb, commute, pass, sail

Expressions: How do you get from / to (your house) to / from (the supermarket)?
How far is it?   How long does it take?

1 (4.3) Listen and circle the correct type of transport.

1 bike / motorbike
2 plane / bike
3 bus / car
4 bus / train

p.55 **2** Choose the correct options to complete the dialogues.

A: How can I get (1)_____ the museum (2)_____ here?

B: You can go (3)_____ bus.

C: How (4)_____ get to your house?

D: You can (5)_____ the train.

E: How (6)_____ does it take you to get to work?

F: It (7)_____ about ten minutes.

1	**a** from	**b** by		**c** to
2	**a** to	**b** from		**c** by
3	**a** on	**b** by		**c** in
4	**a** do you	**b** go you		
5	**a** take	**b** go		
6	**a** far	**b** long		
7	**a** takes	**b** goes		

3 Look at the pictures and complete the sentences.

1 Mr Brown usually _____ to work.

2 Bob Brown _____ to school every day.

3 Mrs Brown _____ to the hairdresser's every week.

4 Sandra Brown _____ to the sports club on Sundays.

4 (4.4) Listen to Matthew, Ravi and Sophie. Who travels:

1 by train?   *Matthew / Ravi / Sophie*
2 by bicycle?   *Matthew / Ravi / Sophie*
3 by car?   *Matthew / Ravi / Sophie*
4 on foot?   *Matthew / Ravi / Sophie*

5 Complete the sentences from Exercise 4 with the correct adjectives. Then listen again and check.

1 I prefer to cycle. It's c _ _ _ _ and h _ _ _ _ _ _ _.
2 Walking is a g _ _ _ _ way to get around, and it's g _ _ _ for me.
3 The trains are c _ _ _ _ _ _ and e _ _ _ _ _ _ _ _.

6 Write T (true) or F (false). Listen and check.

1 Matthew works in London. ___
2 It takes him ten minutes on the train. ___
3 He likes cycling. ___
4 Ravi works at home. ___
5 He hasn't got a car. ___
6 He never walks to the supermarket. ___
7 Sophie likes travelling by train. ___
8 Sophie goes to work by bus. ___

The perfect holiday

Vocabulary

Nouns: attractions, audio file, autumn, podcast, seasons, spring, summer, winter
Verbs: advertise, decide, plan, promote

Test yourself on Unit 4

1 Do these exercises to check your progress.

2 Count your **correct** answers.
Write the total number in the box.

Total: [ ] /46 correct answers

3 Try to understand your mistakes. If necessary,
- read the **Essential Grammar**, and/or
- look at the Student Book lesson again, or
- ask your teacher.

4 How do you feel after this unit? Tick (✓) a box.

👍👍 ☐   👍 ☐   ✊ ☐   👎 ☐   👎👎 ☐

I can ask questions about the future. (Lesson 4F)

1 Put the words in the correct order to make
questions.

1 travel / Where / you / to / going / are / to / ?

_____

2 with / Who / stay / going / are / to / you / ?

_____

3 get / she / How / going / there / is / to / ?

_____

4 hotel / Which / at / are / stay / going / to / they / ?

_____

5 for / is / long / he / How / going / stay / to / ?

_____

6 to / fly / are / Where / you / to / going / ?

_____

2 Complete the answers with *be* and a preposition.
Then match them with the questions in Exercise 1.

a [ ] I___ going to fly _____ Bangkok airport.

b [ ] He___ going to stay _____ three weeks.

c [ ] She___ going there _____ bus.

d [ ] We___ going to stay _____ my aunt and uncle.

e [ ] We___ going to travel _____ India.

f [ ] They___ going to stay _____ the International
Plaza hotel.

I can use have to to talk about obligations. (Lesson 4A)

3 Look at the chart and complete the texts with
have / has to or *don't / doesn't have to*.

Jake	✓	✗	✗	✓
Laura and Carl	✗	✓	✓	✗

1 Jake *has to hoover the floor.*

2 Jake _____

3 Jake _____

4 Jake _____

5 Laura and Carl _____

6 Laura and Carl _____

7 Laura and Carl _____

8 Laura and Carl _____

I can talk about quantities using a, an, some, any.
(Lesson 4B)

4 Complete the sentences with *a(n), some* or *any*.

1 A Would you like _____ toast?
   B Yes, please. And _____ cereal too, if possible.

2 A Do you want _____ sandwich?
   B No, thanks.

3 A Do we have _____ carrots?
   B No, we don't. I didn't buy _____ this week.

4 A Would you like _____ bacon with your eggs?
  B Yes, please.

5 A Is there _____ cheese in the fridge?
  B Yes, there's _____ .

6 A Are there _____ biscuits in the box?
  B No, there aren't.

7 A Do we have _____ eggs in the house?
  B Yes, we do. I bought _____ this morning.

> *I can make, accept and refuse invitations.* **Lesson 4C**

5 Complete the dialogues with the expressions in the box.

> Sorry, I can't   Let's play next weekend, then!
> That would be nice   No, thanks   Would you like to
> we could have a party at home

1 A: Sorry, I can't play tennis with you this week.
  B: _____
  A: OK! I'm free on Sunday morning.

2 A: _____
    have dinner with me tonight?
  B: I'd love to. _____ .

3 A: Can you come to my party next Saturday?
  B: _____ .
    It's my brother's wedding.

4 A: Let's go to the Chinese restaurant near your house.
  B: _____ .
    I don't like Chinese food.

5 A: There's nothing to do in this town. It's boring.
  B: Well, _____ .
  A: Good idea. Let's call all our friends now!

> *I can talk about future plans.* **Lesson 4D**

6 Read Gabriel's plans and complete his e-mail.

> visit friends in Sydney ✓
> travel to Asia ✓
> write a book ✓
> watch a lot of TV ✗
> have Spanish lessons with my neighbour ✓
> swim once a week ✓
> stay at home at the weekend ✗

Dear Mark

Well, I'm going to retire next month. Can you believe it? I know I'm only 50, but this is what I want to do and I've got lots of exciting plans. It's going to be great!

First, I (1)_____ some friends in Sydney. We (2)_____ to Asia together. When I get home, I (3)_____ a book. I'm going to call it … I don't know yet! I plan to keep fit. I (4)_____ once a week. I (5)_____ Spanish lessons. My neighbour (6)_____ me. I'm not going to be lazy. I'm going to make plans for every weekend. I (7)_____ stay at home and I (8)_____ TV!! Well, those are the plans!! Ask me in a year how it's going! And please come and visit one weekend.

Love, Gabriel

> *I can ask and answer about means of transport.*
> **Lesson 4E**

7 Complete the questions about travel to Paris.

1 How do you _____ from Le Bourget airport to the centre of Paris?

2 How _____ does it take by coach from Orly airport to the centre?

3 How _____ is it from Le Bourget airport to the centre of Paris?

4 Can you _____ a coach from Orly airport to the centre?

5 How long _____ to get from Charles de Gaulles airport to the centre by RER train?

> *I can say 50 more words in English.* **Lessons 4A–4F**

8 Cover the words and test yourself on …

1 **WB** Housework (p.74)
Can you remember five jobs around the house with *do*?
Can you remember eight other jobs around the house?

2 **WB** Supermarket (p.75)
Can you remember six fruits and vegetables?

3 **WB** Time (p.76)
Can you spell the months and days and pronounce them with the correct stress?

4 **WB** Prepositions (p.69)
Can you remember 12 prepositions of movement?

5 **Phrasebook 4** (p.78) Look at your translations. Can you say the phrases in English?

Student book

(1.2) 1A Exercise 4

Ewa: … Ms. I'm not married.
Man: What nationality are you?
Ewa: I'm Polish.
Man: And what do you do, Ewa?
Ewa: I'm a student. I study Computer Science.
Man: That's nice. I hope you have a great holiday in Malta. It's very nice here. And, what's your date of birth?
Ewa: Twenty-five, oh-three, nineteen ninety-one.
Man: OK, and what's your address, please.
Ewa: Forty-nine, Zdrojowa Street.
Man: Sorry?
Ewa: It's difficult for you, I know. Zdrojowa. That's Z-D-R-O-J-O-W-A Street.
Man: And where's that?
Ewa: In Lodz.
Man: Wooj?
Ewa: Yes, L-O-D-Z.
Man: Hmm. Polish isn't very easy, is it?
Ewa: For me it is! My problem is with English!
Man: OK, and what's your post code?
Ewa: 90432 PL.
Man: Thank you. That's PL for Poland?
Ewa: Yes.
Man: And what's your phone number please, Ewa?
Ewa: I don't have a phone number here, but my mobile number is 02374 55012.
Man: And what's your email, please?
Ewa: EWAthegreat at yahoo dot com.
Man: And what languages do you speak?
Ewa: Polish, and a little English.
Man: Your English is very good. What do you like doing in your free time, Ewa?
Ewa: I love water sports – that's why I'm here. I love water-skiing and windsurfing.
Man: Great! Malta is perfect for water sports. And why do you want to learn English, Ewa?
Ewa: For my job. After university I want to work in computing and everybody uses English. And I want to travel, too, so English is essential for me.
Man: And finally, what are your reasons for choosing Malta?
Ewa: Well, the weather, the water sports and it's cheap. Oh and one of my friends studies here. She says it's very good.
Man: Thank you very much, Ewa.

(1.6) 1B Exercise 5

Mel: Hi, Jane, I'm sorry I'm late!
Jane: It's almost eight o'clock! Where are you?
Mel: I'm in the car! The traffic is terrible! I'm sitting in a traffic jam.
Jane: Where are you exactly?
Mel: I'm in Harley Street. I'll be there in ten minutes!
Jane: All right. See you then!

Nick: Hello!
Jane: Hey! What are you doing? Where are you?
Nick: Hey, Jane! What's up? I'm at the gym. Where are you?
Jane: At the Dickens Inn! I'm waiting for you! What are you doing at the gym?
Nick: I'm running, you know, on one of those machines … The Dickens Inn …
Jane: Yes, the Dickens Inn! Remember? My birthday dinner?

Nick: Oh, no! Yes, oh… of course! I'm sor… Hey, Jane, happy birthday! What time is the dinner again?
Jane: It was at half past seven … Are you coming?
Nick: Yes, I am! Just give me half an hour!
Jane: OK, take your time… Bye.

Ben: Hello!
Jane: Hi. It's me, Jane!
Ben: Hey, Jane! Happy birthday!
Jane: Thanks. Are you coming to the dinner?
Ben: Of course! I'm having a shower now and then I'll be there!
Jane: Having a shower? So that's, like, an hour before you get here…
Ben: Yes, exactly, see you at 9!
Jane: But we agreed 7.30!
Ben: Oh, really? Er… OK, so I'll hurry! Bye!

Kim: Hi, Jane! How are you!
Jane: How I am? … How am I? Let's see… Angry?!? Are the two of you coming to my birthday dinner or not?
Kim: Sure! We're waiting for a bus right now! The problem is there's an accident and there aren't any buses … I'm very sorry, Jane!
Jane: Never mind! See you later – I hope!

Juan: Hello!
Jane: Hello! Juan? Can you hear me? It's me, Jane!
Juan: Jane who?
Jane: I can't believe it! You're sleeping! It's me, Jane! Jane, from Italy, remember? Your friend?!
Juan: Oh, Jane … Hi… I'm … I'm just waking up … What time is it?
Jane: It's ten to eight in the evening! It's time for dinner, remember?
Juan: Dinner, what dinner? Oh, yes … it's somebody's birthday today, isn't it? … Who is it, do you know?
Jane: Oh!
Juan: Hello? Jane, are you there?

(1.8) 1B Exercise 9

1
Man: Hi darling. I'm on the train. I'm arriving in London. Where are you? OK. Good. Right I'm coming into Victoria. See you in five minutes, darling. OK. Love you. Bye!

2
Woman: He's very ill. doctor. He's very hot. He has a high temperature.
Doctor: Oh dear. Tommy. How are you feeling now?
Tommy: Not very good, doctor.
Doctor: OK. Tommy come here. Can you open and say Ah!
Tommy: Ahh!

3
TV: And it's Ronaldo.
Woman: Yes!
TV: To Rooney.
Woman: Yes, yes!
TV: To Ronaldo.
Woman: Go on!
TV: To Rooney.
Woman: Yes!
TV: Goal!
Woman: Yeeeeeeees!

4
Woman: Can you hear me? Yes, OK. And can you see me? No? OK … I'm moving the camera. Now, can you see me? Yes? Good. I can see you, too. You look great!

(1.12) 1C Exercise 5

Max: I'm a student. I'm doing a Master's … in English. I'm reading a lot of books, so I don't have any free time. That's why I don't have a job. Er, I have some money – my savings. I only spend money on essential things. Er, I don't have any credit cards, I always pay cash. And, I don't have any money for CDs, the cinema, you know, entertainment. But that's fine. I'm broke, but very happy.
Jo: I'm a stay-at-home mother … with four young children. I give them some pocket money each week, but not a lot. They need to learn how much things cost. I have a lot of bills but I always pay on time. That's essential. If not, you work all your life just to pay the banks. Oh, and I never borrow money from friends. I think that's a terrible idea.
Sara: I'm a lawyer. I have a lot of money. And I have some savings, too. I save 20% of my salary every month. That's because I don't want any problems when I retire. I love shopping … for clothes. DVDs, everything. And I always ask for a discount. Well, if you don't ask, you don't get! They usually say no. But sometimes I get a 10% discount for cash. That makes me feel really good!

(1.19) 1E Exercise 6

There's only one problem.
There's Harrods.
There are over 200 museums.
There are many Information Centres.
There are about 50 theatres.
There are lots of lovely street markets.
There are hundreds of excellent restaurants.

(1.21) 1F Exercise 2

Driver: Good morning. Where can I take you?
Tourist: Hi! Yes. The Hotel Majestic, please. It's near Trafalgar Square, opposite the tube station.
Driver: I know it. It looks really nice from the outside.
Tourist: It's nice inside, too!
Driver: Is this your first time in London?
Tourist: Yes. And I love it, but I've only got three days!
Driver: Have you got any friends or family here?
Tourist: My daughter lives in London. She's got a flat near the river.
Driver: Oh, very nice!
Tourist: Yes, it's lovely, but very small. And she's very busy. I have dinner with her every evening, but she works all day. What are the best places to see in this area? Have you got any suggestions?
Driver: Well, we've got some good museums and galleries around here.
Tourist: Yes, but it's very easy to get lost!
Driver: Ah. Have you got a map?
Tourist: I've got a map, but it's quite small.
Driver: Well, you can get good maps from a Tourist Information Centre.
Tourist: Really? Is there one near my hotel?

Audioscript

Driver: Yes, there's one in the road behind your hotel. It's between the bank and a café. You can get a good map there.
Tourist: Thanks. That's a really good idea.
Driver: Uh-huh. OK. This is your hotel. And look – there's a doorman outside the hotel. He can direct you to the Information Centre.
Tourist: One last question! Are there any good English restaurants near here?
Driver: Good question! My favourite is the 'London Choice'. It's very near the Tourist Information Centre.
Tourist: Brilliant! How much is that?
Driver: That will be six pounds fifty.
Tourist: Here you are.
Driver: Have you got any change?
Tourist: That's OK. Keep the change. And thanks for your advice!
Taxi Driver: Uh-huh!

 Revision 1 Exercise 8

OK. Are you ready to play Clothes Bingo? Right, so tick the clothes you hear when I say them. All right? And, when you tick all five, say Bingo! Here's number 1. A shirt. A shirt. Next, we have jeans. And a T-shirt. That's jeans, shirt and T-shirt. And now it's … shoes. And tights. And trainers. That's shoes, tights and trainers. OK. Has anybody got Bingo? No? OK, so let's go on. Now we have a sweater. A sweater. And a top. A top. And a dress. No Bingos? Are you asleep? Come on! The next one is socks. Socks. And a coat. A coat. And a jacket. Now it's skirt. No Bingo? Why not? OK, so let's finish quickly OK, next one – a suit. And trousers. That's suit and dress … and shorts! And ..

 2A Exercise 3

Host: Welcome to Superminds! Mark and Jen are here to answer five memory questions … and win fifty thousand pounds! Hello Mark! Hello Jen!
Mark / Jen: Hi! / Hello!
Host: OK, then! Let's start! Can you remember three facts about the actor, Heath Ledger? You have 20 seconds!
Mark: Heath Ledger? Was he American?
Jen: No, he was Australian. He was the Joker in the film *The Dark Knight*. I liked him. He was very good-looking!
Mark: I know! But that's not a fact.
Host: Right! That's two things – just one more. Only five more seconds.
Jen: Er, I remember! He died on my birthday. On January 22nd, 2008. In New York!
Host: Correct! Well done! Now a question about a celebrity who is alive! This morning on KTla News – that's KTla News – Wow! which American woman said this? 'We weren't lovers when Brad and Jennifer were married. We were just friends!'
Mark: Was it Gisele Bundchen?
Jen: No, it wasn't. She isn't American! It was Angelina Jolie! But I don't believe her!
Host: Great! And now a question about an animal celebrity! This is about the first animal in space!
Jen: Oh – I know – it was a dog.
Mark: And it was Russian!
Host: Correct! But that isn't the question! The question is – what was the dog's name?
Jen: Er – I think it was – La – La something.
Mark: Lara? Was it Lara, Jen?
Jen: No – Lara was in the book *Doctor Zhivago*. No, it was La – Lai– yes – Laika!

Host: You're right! The first animal in space was a dog, Laika! Well done! Well done! The next question is about Diana, Princess of Wales. Where were the Princess and Dodi Al Fayed, her boyfriend, when they died in 1997, in a car accident?
Mark: Was she with him in London, Jen?
Jen: No! They were in Paris, in France.
Host: Right! And now a music question. Who wasn't a member of The Beatles? Was it George, Ringo, David, Paul or John?
Jen: Can you repeat that please?
Host: Yes – George, Ringo, David, Paul or John?
Jen: Well – I remember John Lennon. And Paul McCartney still sings today. Ringo was definitely a Beatle – you can't forget that name!
Mark: So David or George?
Jen: I think George was a Beatle. So, the answer to who wasn't a Beatle is David!
Host: Congratulations! You win fifty thousand pounds!

 2B Exercise 7

A short history of domestic technology.
In the 1920s there were the first electric irons and vacuum cleaners. Then, in the 1930s there were the first automatic washing machines. Hmm. Imagine the changes for women! In the 1940s, there was the first cheap domestic air conditioning. Imagine life without that! In the 1950s, there were rock'n'roll records and music changed completely, too.

In the 1960s there were the first cheap colour TVs and microwaves, and in the 1970s the first commercial dishwashers, and there was stereo radio, too. After that, in the 1980s there were many, many new things, for example the first personal stereos and then the first commercial emails. In the 1990s there were the first laptops and then digital cameras. And in the early 2000s there was wireless internet, or wifi as we now call it. Hm! What do you think is coming next?

 2C Exercise 1

1 Thank you sir. Here's your boarding card. Gate 17.
2 Taxi! Take me to the airport, please. I'm in a hurry!
3 Good morning. Can I see your boarding card, please?
4 Can I have a ticket for the next flight to Beijing?
5 Thanks a lot. Here you are. Keep the change!
6 Good afternoon everybody. Er … Very sorry to be late.
7 Oh no! The flight is one hour late, again!

 2D Exercise 7

Bella was born on the 3rd of July, 1982.
She started school in September, 1987.
She got her first moped when she was 16.
She left school when she was 18.
She went abroad for the first time when she was 19.
She met her partner when she was 21.
She graduated from university in 2003.
She got her first job when she was 22.
She got married on the 1st of February, 2008
She had a baby on the 1st of February, 2009.

 2E Exercise 6

Bob Marley was born in Jamaica on 6th

February, 1945. He was a reggae singer and songwriter, and he wrote that famous song "No Woman, No Cry". He played the guitar.

In the 1960s and 70s he worked with the Wailers, and he sang with his wife and children, too. Bob Marley had 13 children. He smoked and he loved playing football. He died of cancer in a Miami hospital at the age of 37. He gave reggae a universal audience.

 2F Exercise 6

Mel: How about you? Did you have a good weekend?
Tom: It was all right.
Mel: Did you go out on Friday night?
Tom: No, I stayed in. I was really tired. I just watched TV.
Mel: Were you alone?
Tom: Yes, why?
Mel: Oh nothing. Er, what did you do on Saturday?
Tom: In the morning I studied for a test, and then I tidied my flat in the afternoon.
Mel: Uh-huh!
Tom: And on Saturday night, I was online all night – chatting with a girl from Brazil.
Mel: Hmm! What time did you go to bed?
Tom: About half past 3, I think.
Mel: Oh, well… What about Sunday, then? Did you stay in?
Tom: No! I finally went out! On Sunday morning I went shopping. Then I met some friends and we went for a run in the country.
Mel: Great!
Tom: Yes. And in the evening we had a dinner party. I cooked for everybody!
Mel: What did you have to eat?
Tom: Spaghetti Bolognese!
Mel: Wow! Would you like to come and cook for me some time?

 Revision 2 Exercise 3

My first job was in a café. I was a waiter. It wasn't a big café. There were 10 tables inside and in the summer there were five tables outside. too. There were two waiters and one waitress. Oh yes, and one chef. It was an Italian café and there was a picture of the Italian football team on the wall! The food in the café was excellent. There were sandwiches, biscuits and cakes but there weren't any large meals. It was only for drinks and snacks and it was quite cheap. There were always a lot of students and that was fun. It was a good job but now I work in a big hotel in London. It's completely different!

 3A Exercise 3

Dana: Toni? Is that you? Can you hear me? Are you OK?
Toni: Hi Dana. I'm fine. Look it's nothing serious. It's just that – well, thanks for the photo you sent me – but I think it's the wrong one!
Dana: You're joking!
Toni: No, seriously! I wanted the photo from Mayflower Gardens. You know, when we were in Wales.
Dana: What do you mean? I sent you the Mayflower Gardens photo.
Toni: I don't think so. When we were in Mayflower Gardens, there were lots of students.
Dana: That's right. So, which photo did I send you? I hope it's nothing personal!!
Toni: No, no. You're OK! In this photo, well, there

are a lot of families relaxing in a park.

Dana: Uh-huh! Er, is there a river on the left?

Toni: Yup, and, um, there are people swimming in it.

Dana: They're not in boats?

Toni: No. There are some people sitting on the grass and talking. And there's a young guy playing the guitar.

Dana: OK, I think I remember. Er, is there a beautiful woman lying on the grass?

Toni: There are lots of people lying on the grass. There are three people having a picnic. And there's a man standing by a tree. He's looking at the river. Oh – yes, and there are two children playing with a ball.

Dana: You're right. That's not Mayflower Gardens. That's Jupiter Park. I took it last month. Sorry!

Toni: No problem. It's a great photo, and Jupiter Park looks really nice!

Dana: It is. Keep it if you want! And don't worry. I'll email you Mayflower Gardens right now! OK? Thanks for calling.

Toni: Brilliant. Thanks a lot. Take care and speak soon. Bye!

3.4 3B Exercise 4

Kate: OK, guys, here are the answers to the quiz! Are you ready?

Tim: Yeah, go on.

Kate: Right. Number one: it says here it's a very good idea to drink about six glasses of water a day.

Anna: Aha! I got that right!

Kate: Number two: it is very important to sleep a minimum of eight hours a day.

Tim: Really? Eight hours! I had no idea.

Kate: Well, it's what the doctor says ... And number 3 ... The ideal is a minimum of three meals a day.

Anna: Good! Got that one right, too!

Kate: And next: it's excellent for the mind to read about two books a month, or to watch about two good films.

Tim: Two books a month? I read about four!!!

Leo: Really? Where do you find the time? What else, Kate?

Kate: Number six is no surprise: eating a lot of chocolate is bad for you... So a box of chocolates a week is crazy! Now... this is a surprise!

Tim: What?

Kate: It's very good for you to drink about six or seven cups of coffee a day!!!

Leo: Really? Hmmm... Coffee? Good for you? You can't be serious...

Kate: Well, this is what Doctor Woods says, not me... And number 8 is another surprise: doing exercise once a week only doesn't make any difference for your health! And number 9 is a nice surprise: a glass of wine every evening is very good for you!

Leo: Hey! Really! That's excellent news!

Anna: Hey, Leo. She said a glass of wine every evening, not a bottle!!! A bottle every evening is bad for you!

Leo: And what about number 10?

Kate: Smoking? What do you think? You know smoking is bad for you!!! 100 cigarettes or one cigarette! It's always bad for you!

Leo: OK, OK...

3.6 3C Exercise 4

Tim: ... very interesting. Now, about your computer skills. Could you tell me something about your computer skills, please, Jo?

Jo: OK. Well, I can type quite fast. When I first started at college I couldn't type very fast at all – in fact I could only type with two fingers! Now, I'm much better! I can create spreadsheets, I can install software very well, ...

Tim: Well, what can you do on a computer?

Jo: Sure. What would you like to know?

Anna: Can you use a scanner?

Jo: Yes, I can! Well, I think I can. I never used one, but it's easy, isn't it?

Anna: So is the answer yes or no?

Jo: No, I guess the answer is no. No, I can't use a scanner ... but it isn't difficult, I know.

Tim: OK. Can you prepare PowerPoint presentations?

Jo: Oh, yes, I can! Very well! I love playing with PowerPoint.

Anna: Good! Can you speak Spanish?

Jo: Si, hablo muy bien español.

Tim: Could you have a phone conversation in Spanish? You know, talk to our offices in South America and Mexico, take messages ...

Jo: Yes, sure. Well, I could about five years ago. I lived in Spain when I was a child. I spoke Spanish all the time. I just need a bit of practice.

Tim: OK, good. And what about e-mails ... can you write e-mails in English and Spanish?

Jo: In English, yes, for sure. My writing in Spanish isn't that good. I need a dictionary.

Anna: That's no problem. Now, your CV shows that you ...

3.9 3D Exercise 5

1 Charles can ride a horse very well.
2 Camilla can speak Spanish quite well.
3 My father eats quite slowly.
4 My mother doesn't drive carefully.
5 I sing very, very badly.

3.13 3F Exercise 4

Pam: It was terrible. I was on my own in Chicago at night with no hotel room. I was so angry!

Martin: You know, this problem happens a lot with big hotels.

Pam: Really?

Martin: Yeah. They overbook because they know some people usually cancel or just don't arrive.

Pam: What!

Martin: Yeah. They want a full hotel so they say that there are rooms available when there aren't!

Pam: So, they're lying! What can I do, Martin? Can I get compensation?

Martin: Well, did you stay at the hotel they suggested?

Pam: Yes – and it was terrible.

Martin: Then – write to them. Write a really angry e-mail. My brother had the same problem last year with a hotel in London. He wrote a very angry letter and they gave him a free weekend at a five-star hotel.

Pam: Hmm ...

Martin: So, Pam tell me what happened at the hotel.

Pam: Well, um, first., er I got my room key ...

3.18 3F Exercise 9

Pam: Well, first, the room was on the sixth floor and the lift didn't work!

Martin: Oh no!

Pam: The room was very small and there wasn't a shower, only a bath. And the water was cold! Oh yes, the TV didn't work so I couldn't watch the news. And the kettle in the room didn't work, so I couldn't make a cup of coffee.

Martin: Anything else?

Pam: Yes – the heating. I couldn't turn it off. And I couldn't open the window, so it was really hot.

Martin: But, was the room clean?

Pam: No. It was dirty. And another thing – it was really expensive!

Martin: When are you going to write that e-mail?

Pam: Right now!

3.19 Revision 3 Exercise 3

I think I'm quite healthy really! I mean, I drink at least 8 glasses of water a day and I do a lot of exercise every week. I don't smoke very much. Only three cigarettes a day and I have three cups of coffee in the morning. That's not a lot, is it? I drink one glass of wine with my dinner, but just one. Oh, and I always take my dog to the park for half an hour after work. So, yes, I think I'm OK. Hm?

4.2 4A Exercise 4

Joe: Good evening, ladies and gentlemen ... Here with us tonight we have Sally Welles, author of this month's bestseller, *Wear Two Hats and Be Cool*. Hello, Sally.

Sally: Good evening, Joe. Good evening, everyone. Er, thank you!

Joe: So Sally, what are these 'two hats'?

Sally: Well, Joe, they represent the two roles women play in modern society. We have to wear the Family hat ... and the Professional hat.

Joe: I see. Can you give us some examples?

Sally: Sure. As a mother, there are many things I have to do. Not that I want to do them, but I have no choice. For example, I have to do the housework. You know, ... I have to clean, and wash, and tidy up. Also, I have to do the shopping for the family, and because I really like being a mother and cooking for my children, I have to prepare their meals, especially their breakfast.

Joe: And at the same time you have your professional life ...

Sally: That's it. Wearing my professional hat I have to go to meetings almost every day. And sometimes I have to start work early you know, because that's the only way to get time to do everything. And very often I have to see people all day.

Joe: Sure. And do you have to travel a lot on business?

Sally: No, not really. My office is near my house and I write at home so ...

4.3 4A Exercise 5

Joe: And are you still married, Sally?

Sally: No, no, I'm not. My husband died two

years ago. Yes, it was very sad. But I have a boyfriend. And my parents help me a lot.

Joe: That's nice. How do they help you?

Sally: Well, in the mornings, for example, I don't have to take the children to school, because my father does that every day. He's great.

Joe: So you work a lot, you work all day, at home and at your office. Do you ever have time for yourself?

Sally: Oh, yes, certainly. And I have to see my boyfriend sometimes ..., you know ...

4.12 4C Exercise 7

1 Would you like to go shopping this afternoon?
2 Would you like to go for a walk tomorrow?
3 Would you like to come to my house for dinner this weekend?
4 Would you like to borrow my new Ferrari?
5 Would you like to wash my car?

4.14 4D Exercise 3

Zoe: The show was great last week, wasn't it?

Jay: Wonderful! I love musicals. Let's go out again next weekend!

Zoe: I'd love to, but I can't. I'm going to visit my brother in Australia.

Jay: Australia! Wow! How long are you going to stay there?

Zoe: Three weeks.

Jay: Nice! Are you going to do anything special?

Zoe: Yes, we are. Charlie ...

Jay: We ...? Charlie?

Zoe: Charlie! My brother, Charlie. He lives in Sydney.

Jay: Lucky you! I hear it's great.

Zoe: Yes, Charlie says it's brilliant. But we aren't going to be there long.

Jay: No? Why not?

Zoe: We're only going to stay in Sydney for three days. Then we're going to fly up to Queensland.

Jay: Mmm. Queensland?

Zoe: Yup! We're going to go scuba-diving on the Great Barrier Reef.

Jay: Oh! Wow! Are you going to be careful? I mean, there are lots of sharks!

Zoe: I know. I love sharks. That's why I want to go!

4.17 4D Exercise 7

Ben: Hi Mark. Have you got any plans for the weekend?

Mark: No, I'm going to stay in. I'm really tired.

Ben: So, you don't want to go out this evening?

Mark: No way. I'm going to relax.

Ben: Hmm, nice. Is Sandy going to come round?

Mark: No, she works on Friday nights.

Ben: Uh-huh. So, what are you going to do?

Mark: I don't know. It depends. Watch TV. Maybe read a bit, then go to bed. OK?

Ben: Hiya Sophie. It's Ben. How are you?

Sophie: Oh. Hi Ben, yeah – I'm fine, thanks.

Ben: Good. Look Sophie. Are you going to be here next weekend?

Sophie: No, sorry. I'm going to go away.

Ben: Are you? Right. Where exactly?

Sophie: Up to the mountains. I'm going to stay in a small town with some friends.

Ben: OK. So, Sophie, er, what are you going to do with your friends?

Sophie: I'm not sure. Eat a lot, you know, the usual. It depends on the weather ...

Ben: How long are you going to be there?

Sophie: Only two nights. I have to work on Monday! Sorry, Ben. I have to go. See you. Bye!

Ben: Oh!

4.18 4E Exercise 4

Charlie: So, are you ready to come?

Zoe: Nearly! I just have to pack. But, I'm a bit scared. It's a long flight!

Charlie: Don't worry. Just sleep on the plane.

Zoe: OK. I can't wait to see you again!

Charlie: Me too. But, er, listen. Sorry, Zoe, but I'm afraid I can't meet you at the airport.

Zoe: Oh, really? Why not?

Charlie: There's going to be a really important meeting at work! I have to go.

Zoe: But Charlie! I thought you were on holiday!

Charlie: I am! But this is an emergency! I have to be there.

Zoe: OK. So how do I get to your house from the airport? I'm very scared now.

Charlie: Don't worry! It's really easy. There's an underground station at the airport. Take the train to the city centre. Then you can get a taxi to my place. It only takes about ten minutes.

Zoe: Can't I walk from the station?

Charlie: Not with luggage, no.

Zoe: How far is it?

Charlie: It's exactly two kilometres. But get a taxi. They're not very expensive.

Zoe: Oh, Charlie. Are you sure? You know it's my first trip abroad!

Charlie: Don't worry, Zoe! They speak English here you know. Everything is going to be alright. We're going have a wonderful time!

4.21 4F Exercise 5

Zoe: Hello everybody. This is my first podcast! It has some great websites for travellers. I hope you enjoy it! ... And with me is my friend Jay. Say hello, Jay.

Jay: Hi Zoe. Hello everybody.

Zoe: So, Jay. For your next holiday, where are you going to travel to?

Jay: I'm going to visit Thailand.

Zoe: Wow! How long are you going to stay there?

Jay: For a month.

Zoe: Great! How are you going to get there?

Jay: By plane. I found some cheap flights on the Net. Really cheap. And they're direct!. The site is travelocity.com

Zoe: Travelocity? One word?

Jay: Yeah.

Zoe: Cheap direct flights – that's good to know! And what are you going to do when you arrive?

Jay: Visit Bangkok. I found some great tips on the Net. There's a great site: www.virtualtourist.com

Zoe: Is that V-I-R-T-U-A-L tourist?

Jay: Yes, one word, virtualtourist.com

Zoe: Uh-huh And how are you going to get around?

Jay: By tuk-tuk. Or rent a motorbike. Both are really cheap.

Zoe: Where are you going to stay?

Jay: I can't remember the hotel name – but I got a great deal from asiarooms.com

Zoe: Asiarooms? One word?

Jay: Yes, asiarooms.com

Zoe: And, who are you going to go with?

Jay: You! I hope?

Zoe: What?

Jay: Yes, you. Please? Please come with me, Zoe.

Zoe: Oh Jay. Wow! Er, that's great! I don't know what to say. Thank you!

Jay: I bought you a ticket. Look!

Zoe: Er, you're very kind, Jay. But, er, can I think about it for a day or two?

Activity book

1.6 1E Exercise 3

Man: Excuse me. Is there an underground station ... sorry, I mean a tube station ... near here?

Woman: Yes ... there's one opposite the bookshop down this street.

Man: Near the bookshop ... I'm not sure where the bookshop is.

Woman: OK. Can you see the hairdresser's?

Man: Yes.

Woman: Well, next to the hairdresser's is the library and then next to the library is the bookshop and the tube is opposite.

Man: Thanks. And I also need to go to a cashpoint.

Woman: There's a cashpoint between the bookshop and the chemist's.

Man: Great. Thank you very much.

Woman: No problem. Enjoy your holiday.

2.2 2B Exercise 4

1 When I was young, there were only black and white televisions.
2 When I was a boy, there were lots of bikes and horses, but no cars.
3 When I was a child, there were three phones in our house, but there weren't any mobiles.
4 There was no internet when my parents were teenagers.
5 When I was a boy, there were public phones everywhere. There weren't any mobiles in those days.

2.5 2E Exercise 1

1

Woman A: Did you hear that concert by The Killers on the radio last night? It was fantastic. The Killers are great. I love their music.

2

Male: No, I think it's terrible! The Killers are boring. Their songs are all the same.

Woman A: Well, what do you think? Do you like the Killers?

3

Woman B: Well, their new song's OK. But I prefer some of their old ones. They're not really my favourite band.

2.6 2F Exercise 1

Anna: Hi Di. It's Anna.

Di: Hi Anna. How was Glastonbury?

Anna: It was fantastic. Wonderful! I really loved it.

Di: So, what did you see?

Anna: Millions of things. Er, let's see. Oh yeah, I saw Bjork. She was amazing!

Di: Lucky you!

Anna: Yeah and I also went to see Jay-Z. He was great. But I didn't get to the El Ritmo for the salsa lessons.

Di: Oh well. Can't do everything.

Anna: No, no, that's impossible. It's enormous.

Di: Did you see Miku and Sanna?

Anna: Yes, I did – they were brilliant. Oh yes and I went to some of the poetry open sessions too.

Di: Wow, interesting. Did you see anybody famous …?

(3.3) 3B Exercise 2

Emma: My name is Emma. I drink a glass orange juice with my breakfast and a glass of water with lunch and dinner. I don't normally drink any alcohol, except on special occasions.
I hate smoking. I don't often eat chocolate, but sometimes my husband buys me a box of chocolates for my birthday. I do lots of exercise, and I never watch TV and I try to sleep eight hours a night.

Oliver: My name is Oliver. I smoke two packets of cigarettes a day, and I drink a bottle of wine every week. I only sleep about five hours a night. I watch TV about five hours a day. I never drink water. I know it's good for me but I don't like it. I drink about eight cups of coffee a day!

(3.4) 3C Exercise 4

Jack: … this is a busy internet café and we all help.

Claire: OK.

Jack: So … cooking. Can you cook?

Claire: Sure! I can cook very well. I can cook sausages, eggs, pasta. I can make coffee, tea ….

Jack: Great. Can you use a computer?

Claire: Yes, I can so I can help people in the café.

Jack: That's great … and can you use a messenger? And can you have a phone conversation on the internet?

Claire: Yeah! Of course. No problem.

Jack: Excellent. Can you drive?

Claire: No, I can't. I can ride a bike …

Jack: No problem. Look, we often have foreign students in the café. Can you speak any other languages?

Claire: Yeah! I can speak Spanish, German, French, Russian …

Jack: Great. That's fantastic. When can you start?

Claire: Today. Now.

Jack: Excellent. I've got a problem with the computer. Can you help?

(3.5) 3D Exercise 1

Bill: I saw a really interesting website about how to learn languages quickly. Do you learn new things quickly, Louise? Or do you find it difficult to learn new skills?

Louise: I find it difficult. I tried singing lessons a few years ago – I sang really badly but I wanted to learn. But it was no good. I couldn't improve. I still sing really badly.

Bill: Oh dear ….

Louise: But I can play the piano. I learned to play when I was a girl. It was easy to learn new things then. And I play very

well because I practise a lot.

Bill: What about languages? Do you learn languages easily?

Louise: Learning languages is very difficult. I can speak a little Spanish, but I can't understand very much so people need to speak slowly to me. I'm better at French. I can understand French easily, and I can speak quite well.

Bill: What do you enjoy learning?

Louise: Well, I like cooking. I like learning new recipes and I always follow them very carefully. And what about you, Bill? Do you learn …

(3.8) 3F Exercise 7

A: Do you know anybody here?

B: I know Ann, over there. Do you know her?

A: Ann? No, I don't think so. Do you mean the girl wearing the green dress?

B: No, not the tall girl. Ann's quite short. She's got blue eyes and is wearing a yellow t-shirt. She's got glasses.

A: Oh, yes, I see. So, who's the tall girl?

B: You mean the very thin girl in the corner. The girl with long black hair?

A: Yes, she's got lovely green eyes, too!

B: Oh, that's Sally, a friend of Dave's. It's his party.

A: Which one is Dave?

B: I can't see him. Well, Dave's medium height. He's got brown eyes and he's wearing black jeans. Oh and he's bald.

A: Is Sally his girlfriend?

B: No, I don't think so!

A: Oh, that's good!

B: Hmmm!

(4.4) 4E Exercise 4

Woman: Excuse me … could I ask you some questions?

Matthew: Sure.

Woman: What's your name and how do you get to work?

Matthew: Matthew. I work in London and it takes me one hour to get there by train, and then I have to walk for ten minutes. The train's often late, so sometimes it takes me an hour and a half. I prefer to cycle. It's cheap and healthy! It only takes about 45 minutes by bike, and I'm getting lots of exercise. I try to cycle every day when the weather is good.

Woman: Excuse me … what about you? How do you get around?

Ravi: I work at home so I don't need to travel very much. I haven't got a car, so I walk or take the bus. It only takes me ten minutes to walk to the shops, and five minutes to walk to the bus station , so you see I don't need a car. Walking is a great way to get around, and it's good for me too.

Woman: Excuse me … What's your name and how do you get to work?

Sophie: Sophie … my name's Sophie. I'm from Paris but I work in London. And I hate public transport. The trains are dirty and very expensive and the buses – huh!… well, you never know when the next bus is going to arrive. So I go to work by bike.

(4.5) Irregular verbs

Infinitive	Past simple
be	was / were
become	became
buy	bought
come	came
do	did
drink	drank
drive	drove
eat	ate
feel	felt
find	found
fly	flew
forget	forgot
get	got
give	gave
go	went
have	had
hear	heard
keep	kept
leave	left
make	made
meet	met
put	put
read /riːd/	read /red/
ride	rode
say	said
see	saw
send	sent
sing	sang
sleep	slept
speak	spoke
spend	spent
take	took
teach	taught
tell	told
think	thought
understand	understood
wake	woke
write	wrote

111

1 Essential Grammar

Articles: *a / an*, *the* or no article → 1A

Singular	This is **an** exercise in a book. This is **the** book I study with.
Plural	**The** exercises help me learn ~~the~~ English.
No article	~~The~~ English grammar is quite easy.

Rules

1 Use indefinite article **a/an** for *singular / plural* nouns when we don't know which one.

2 Use definite article **the** for singular and plural nouns when we *know / don't know* which one.

3 *Use / Don't use* an article when we talk generally or for names of people or countries.

1 Circle the correct rule.

2 Complete the sentences with *a, an, the* or 0 (= no article).

1 _0_ Brazil is ___ big country. It has ___ fantastic beaches and ___ people are very friendly. It's ___ great.

2 ___ Europe is only ___ small continent, but ___ EU is ___ important organisation with ___ lot of power.

3 My brother ___ Marc loves ___ chocolate. He thinks ___ Swiss chocolate is ___ best in ___ world.

To / for → 1A

to + verb	I'm studying this page to practise grammar.
for + noun	I'm learning English for my job.

3 Complete the sentence with *to* or *for*.

We're here ...

1 _for_ a meeting.
2 ____ see the manager.
3 ____ have a good time.
4 ____ meet a friend.
5 ____ an interview.
6 ____ the money.

Present continuous → 1B

I	'm / 'm not	sitting on a chair. wearing a jacket.
You / We / They	're / aren't	
He / She	's / isn't	
❓	Are you / Is he studying a lot?	
✓/✗	Yes, I am. / No, he isn't.	

Verbs NOT usually used in the continuous form:

know   like   need
remember   think (opinion)   understand

✓ Do you like jazz?   ✗ ~~Are you liking jazz?~~

4 Circle the correct rule.

1 Use the Present continuous for actions *we do every day / in progress now*.

2 You *can / can't* use all English verbs in the Present continuous.

5 Write the *–ing* form of the verbs in the correct column.

begin   do   drive   kiss   live   play   run
send   stop   swim   wake up   work   write

+ –ing	–e + –ing	double final consonant
doing	driving	beginning

6 Look at the photo on page 14. Put the verbs in the Present simple or Present continuous.

1 The woman _has_ short black hair and _____ next to the man. (have, stand)

2 She _____ a yellow jacket. She _____ jeans. (wear × 2)

3 The man _____ two bags. (carry).

4 The man _____ the taxi driver. (look at).

A lot (of), some, not any + plural C or U nouns → 1C

Large quantity	I (don't) have **a lot of** coins.
Indefinite quantity	I have **some** notes.
Zero	I don't have **any** money.

7 Choose *a lot of*, *some* or *any* to describe India.

1 _____ people live in India.

2 _____ people in India are really rich but _____ them are very poor.

3 _____ of the poor people don't have electricity.

4 _____ tourists visit the Taj Mahal every year.

5 I don't have _____ brothers or sisters in India.

Pronouns for things → 1D

	Singular	a shirt	Plural	shoes
Subject	It's purple.		They're blue.	
Object	I'll take it.		I'll take them.	
Here or there?	This is / That's a lovely shirt.		These / Those are lovely shoes.	
Don't repeat the noun	I like the red shirt, but I prefer the purple one.		I like the brown shoes, but I prefer the blue ones.	
To ask 'which'	Which one do you prefer?		Which ones do you prefer?	

8 Replace the words in italics in dialogues 1 and 2 with *one*, *ones*, *it*, *they* or *them*.

1 **A:** I love that book.

  B: Which (1)*book*?   *one*

  A: The (2)*book* you have in your hand. _____

  B: Ah, this (3)*book*. Yes, I like (4)*this book*, too. _____ _____

2 **A:** How much are those trousers?

  B: Which (5)*trousers*? The blue (6)*trousers*? _____ _____

  A: No, the grey (7)*trousers*. _____

  B: (8)These *trousers* are 150 euros. _____

  A: Oh! And how much are (9)the blue *trousers*? _____

  B: (10)The blue *trousers* are only 50 euros. _____

  A: OK. I'll take (11)the blue *trousers*. _____ _____

There is / are → 1E, 1F

➕	There's a great shop in this street. There are nice cafés.
➖	There isn't a cash machine. There aren't any big offices.
❓	Is there a post office near here? Are there (any) good banks?
✔/✗	Yes, there is. / No, there isn't. Yes, there are. / No, there aren't.

9 Complete the sentences with *is*, *are*, *aren't*, *a* or *any*.

1 There _____ 12 exercises on this page, there _____ only 11.

2 There _____ _____ photo of _____ man and _____ woman. There _____ _____ photos of animals.

3 '_____ there _____ photos of children?' 'No, there _____ .'

4 '_____ there a photo of _____ taxi?' 'Yes, there _____ .'

5 There _____ a grammar exercise under each grammar box. There _____ answers near the end of this page.

Have got = *have* for possession, but not for activities → 1F

➕	I / You	've		❓	Have you got a laptop?	Has it got wifi?
➖	We / They	haven't	got a computer.	➕	Yes, we have.	Yes, it has.
➕	He / She	's		➖	No, I haven't.	No, it hasn't.
➖	It	hasn't				

10 Possession or activity? Write R (right) or W (wrong). Correct the wrong ones.

1 We've got a small dog. ___   2 It's got big eyes. ___   3 It's got two meals a day. ___

11 This dialogue is correct. But can you rewrite it using *have got*?

A: (1)~~Do you have~~ a boyfriend? *Have you got*

B: (2)Yes, I do. _____

A: (3)Does he have any brothers or sisters?

_____

B: (4)Yes, he has two sisters, but he doesn't have a brother. _____

113

2 Essential Grammar

Past simple: verb be → 2A

+	I / He / She / It	was / wasn't	at home yesterday.
−	You / We / They	were / weren't	
?	Was	he	at work this morning?
	Were	you	
✓	Yes,	he	was. / wasn't.
✗	No,	we	were. / weren't.

Rules

1 The two positive past forms of *be* are _____ and _____ .
2 The two negative forms of *be* are _____ and _____ .
3 _____ is the past of *am* and *is*.
4 _____ is the past of *aren't*.
5 _____ is a contraction of *was not*.
6 _____ is a contraction of *were not*.
7 _____ , _____ and *weren't* have only one syllable.
8 _____ has two syllables /ˈwɒzənt/.

1 Complete the rules of the past forms of *be*.

There *was / were* + C and U nouns → 2B

+	There was satellite TV	in 1990.	
	There were CDs		
−	There	was no / wasn't (any)	internet.
	There	were no / weren't (any)	MP3s.	no = not any
?	Was there	a VCR in your school?	
	Were there (any)	computers?	
✓	Yes, there was. / No, there wasn't.		
✗	Yes, there were. / No, there weren't.		

2 Complete the dialogue with *there was / were*.

S: Dad, (1)_____ electricity in the nineteenth century?

F: Yes, (2)_____ _____ , and (3)_____ _____ radio but (4)_____ _____ no TVs.

S: Really? And (5)_____ _____ any cars?

F: No, (6)_____ _____ . (7)_____ _____ only some simple motorbikes.

S: And Dad, (8)_____ _____ any trains?

F: Yes, (9)_____ _____ a lot of trains in many countries.

Time expressions: Past → 2A, 2B

	yesterday.
	last week (month, year).
Things were different	last Monday (evening, weekend) on Saturday (evening, night) in 1985.
	in the 1980s.
	in the 21st century.
	when I was a child.

3 Complete the sentence with *in*, *in the*, *on*, *a* or no article (0).

They were popular ...

1 _o_ last weekend.
2 ____ 2009.
3 ____ 1990s.
4 ____ last Friday.
5 ____ Friday.
6 ____ month ago.
7 ____ last December.
8 ____ two years ago.
9 ____ when I was 13.
10 ____ 20th century.

Past simple → 2C, 2D, 2E, 2F

Yesterday...

+	I / You / He / She	worked	a lot.
−	It/ We / They	didn't work	yesterday.
?	Did	you work	a lot?
✓	Yes,	I did.	
✗	No,	we didn't.	

Question	**A**uxiliary	**S**ubject	**I**nfinitive
What time		he	go out?
Where	did	they	have dinner?
What		you	do then?

Rule

Word order in questions = **Q A S I**.

114

Regular verbs		Irregular verbs			
Spelling	**Pronunciation**	**Infinitive**	**Past**	hear	_____
work + −ed = work**ed**	***Don't*** pronounce the ***e*** in **−ed**.	become	became	leave	_____
live − e + −ed = liv**ed**	worked	come	came	make	_____
play + −ed = play**ed**	lived	do	did	meet	_____
study − y + **i** + −ed = stud**ied**	studied	forget	forgot	see	_____
stop + **p** + −ed = stop**ped**	***Except*** in verbs ending in **−d** or **−t**.	drive	drove	sell	_____
	board<u>e</u>d	get	got	sing	_____
	start<u>e</u>d	give	gave	speak	_____
		go	went	think	_____
		have	had	write	_____

4 Write T (true) or F (false).

1 All past tense verbs in English end in −ed. ____

2 Positive and negative past tense forms are different for each person. ____

3 The only verb with two irregular past tense forms is the verb *be*. ____

4 Word order in Past simple questions is the same as the Present simple. ____

5 To form questions and negatives in the past tense, we use *did* and *didn't*. ____

6 We <u>always</u> pronounce the letter *e* in the ending −*ed*. ____

7 The past tense forms of *come* and *become* and *get* and *forget* are similar. ____

8 Irregular past tense forms have the same number of syllables as their infinitive. ____

5 Complete the second column of irregular verbs. Check your answer on page 111.

6 Change the story from present to past.

Present

On Fridays, I plan my weekend, and then I stop work early and go home. I arrive home, listen to music and tidy my house. But I don't go out. I relax, watch TV and have dinner on the sofa. And I don't go to bed late.

Past

Last Friday, I planned my weekend, and then I (1)_____ work early and (2)_____ home. I (3)_____ home, (4)_____ to music and (5)_____ my house. But I (6)_____ go out. I (7)_____ , (8)_____ TV and (9)_____ dinner on the sofa. And I (6)_____ go to bed late.

7 What didn't Jo do last year? Write a sentence for each picture.

1 <u>Jo didn't go to university</u>   2 _____   3 _____   4 _____

8 Complete the questions in the dialogue.

A: What (1) _____ _____ _____ last night?

B: I went to the cinema.

A: Who (2)_____ _____ _____ with?

B: With my girlfriend.

A: Which film (3)_____ _____ _____?

B: I can't remember.

A: Oh! Well, (4)_____ _____ enjoy it?

A: It was OK.

B: (5)_____ _____ _____ anything special after that?

A: Not really. We had a quick pizza and came home.

115

Linking ideas to describe what you see → 3A

Present		Past
In the picture	there's a man **talking** on the phone.	Last night **there was** a band **playing** at the end of my road.
In the café	there are some women **having** a drink.	At midnight **there were** a lot of people **singing** and **dancing**.

1 Use the words and pictures to write a sentence.

1 I can see / _____ / park

   I can see two men jogging in the park.

2 Over there /

   Over there, there _____

3 There _____

4 Last night /

   _____ TV.

2 Complete the past tense questions and answers about Exercise 1.

1 ' __Was__ __there__ only one man *running* in the park?' 'No, _____ _____ two.'

2 '_____ _____ a lot of children _____ football?' 'Yes, _____ _____ .'

3 '_____ _____ two women _____ for a bus?' 'No, _____ _____ only _____ .'

4 '_____ _____ a man _____ on TV?' 'No, _____ _____ .'

How much / How many? → 3B

Countable (C)	Uncountable (U)
How many coins do you have?	How much money do you have?
Some. (= not a lot)	Some. (= not a lot)
Four. (=)	A little. (=)
None. (= 0)	None. (= 0)

3 Complete the rules with C or U.

1 Use *How much* for ___ nouns.

2 Use *How many* for ___ nouns.

3 ___ nouns have a plural form.

4 ___ plural forms usually end in –s.

4 Complete the table with *much* or *many*. Write your answers, too.

1	__How many__ T-shirts	do you have?	_____
2	How _____ time		_____
3	How _____ phones	have you got?	_____
4	How _____ cash		_____

5	How _____ water		_____
6	How _____ eggs	did you have for breakfast?	_____
7	How _____ milk		_____
8	How _____ sugar		_____

Can / Could for ability and requests → 3C

➕ ➖	I You He She We They	can could	text
			really / very well.
			(quite) well a bit / a little.
		can't couldn't	ski
			(very) well. (at all).
❓	Can	you	sing well?
			Yes, we can / No, we can't.
	Could		ski five years ago?
			Yes, we could / No we couldn't.

5 Write T (true) or F (false).

1 *Can* and *could* are the same for all persons. ___

2 We normally contract the negative forms *can not* and *could not*. ___

3 *Can't* and *couldn't* both have two syllables. ___

4 *I can't (text) at all = I have no idea (how to text).* ___

5 *Can* and *could* have two meanings: *Can you swim?* (ability) and *Can / Could you open the door please?* (request) ___

6 Match the questions and answers.

1 Can you meet me at six?
2 Could you do the homework?
3 Can you drive?

a No, it was really difficult.
b Yes, a bit. I'm taking lessons.
c Sorry, I'm busy. How about later?

Adverbs → 3D

Adjective	Adverb
What's the **exact** answer?	What **exactly** is the answer?
That answer was **easy**.	I answered **easily**.
Irregular adverbs: good → well fast → fast	

8 Write a similar sentence with a verb + adverb.

1 He's a quick driver.   *He drives quickly.*
2 She's a fast runner.   _____
3 I'm a careful writer.   _____
4 They're good workers.   _____
5 He's a dangerous player.   _____

7 Complete the rules with *adverb* or *adjective*.

Rules

1 An _____ describes a noun.
2 An _____ describes a verb.
3 The usual ending for an _____ is –*ly*.
4 For an _____ ending in -*y*, change the –*y* to –*ily* to make the _____ .
5 *Well* is an irregular _____ .

6 She's a regular listener.   _____
7 We're bad speakers.   _____
8 I'm a happy sleeper!   _____

Describing people: word order → 3E

Faces			Size	Colour	
Singular noun	I have (got) ... She has (got) ...	a(n)	long / big	black brown blue	beard. moustache.
Plural and U Nouns	He doesn't have She hasn't got	ø	short / small		hair. eyes.

9 Circle the correct rule.

1 Size adjectives go *before* / *after* colour.
2 *Beard* and *moustache* are C /U nouns.
3 Use *have* + article + C / U noun.
4 *Hair* is usually C / U.
5 Use *have* + no article + C / U noun.

10 Correct two mistakes in each description.

1 Homer Simpson's got small black eyes and ^'s short and fat.   *he*
2 Marge Simpson quite tall and has blue long hair.
3 Daniel Craig's a medium build and he has blue eyes and short brown hairs.
4 Keira Knightley's tall quite and very thin. She has long brown hair and the dark eyes.

Prepositions → 3F

Use *at / in / on* for position:
Toni's at home, in his bedroom on the first floor.

Use *to* for movement:

I'm driving to work.

11 Complete the sentences with *at, in, on* or *to*.

1 Take the lift ___ to the ninth floor.
2 See you ___ the first floor.
3 Our room is ___ the end ___ the left.
4 I left my key ___ my room.
5 I'm walking ___ the car park.
6 They're waiting ___ the bus stop.

Obligation: *have to* → 4A

⊕ ⊖	I / You We / They	have to don't have to	work today. study.
⊕ ⊖	He / She / It	has to doesn't have to	
❓	Do I	have to	
✔ ✘	Yes, you do. No, you don't.		

1 Circle *O*, *N* or *P*. O = obligation, N = no obligation
(= You can choose), P = possession.

1 I don't have a car.	O N	Ⓟ
2 I have to go now. Bye!	O N	P
3 It's OK, you don't have to come today.	O N	P
4 Sue's feeling happy because she doesn't have to work next week.	O N	P
5 Has Sue got any children?	O N	P
6 We have to drive our mother to hospital after breakfast.	O N	P

Countable (C) and uncountable (U) nouns → 4B

Quantities		C	U
⊕ I'd like	a	sandwich.	XXX
	some	crisps.	cheese.
⊖ We don't need	any	chips.	meat.
❓ Do you have		biscuits?	bread?
Offers and Requests			
Do you want / Would you like		a drink?	some tea?
Can I have / Could you give me		some beans?	some more ice?

2 Write T (true) or F (false).

1 Use *a/an* for C and U nouns. ___

2 Use *some* for C and U nouns. ___

3 Use *any* in questions and negatives for C and U nouns. ___

4 In offers and requests, use *some* for C and U nouns. ___

5 *Some* is positive. Use it in offers and requests to ask politely for something. ___

3 Complete the offer (O) and request (R) for each picture.

1 O Would you li *ke some* water?

2 R Can I ha *ve some* water?

3 O Do you ne___ _____ ?

4 R Can I bo___ _____ ?

5 O Do you wa___ _____ ?

6 R Could you gi___ m__ _____ ?

7 O Would you ___ ___ _____ ?

8 R Can I h___ ___ _____ ?

4 Read situations 1–3. What question do you ask? Match each situation to the correct question, A–C.

1 You're in a shop and know they sell milk.

2 You're in a shop, but don't know if they sell milk. What do you ask?

3 You're in a café. You asked for white coffee, but it's almost black.

A Do you have any milk?

B Can I have some milk, please?

C Can I have some more milk, please?

Invitations → 4C

Inviting	Would you like Do you want	to see a film?
Saying yes	Sure, Yes,	why not? that would be nice! I'd love to.
Saying no	Sorry, I can't. I'd love to, but …	
Asking for a reason	Why? / Why not?	
Giving an excuse	Because I'm busy / tired. I'm finishing my homework. Because I have to work tonight.	

5 Cross out the extra word in each line.

1 A: Would you like to play ~~playing~~ cards?
   B: Sorry, I am can't.
   A: Why you not?
   B: I'm do doing my homework.

2 A: Do you are want to go out tonight?
   B: Yes, that would is be great.
   C: Yes, I'd to love to.
   A: Would you like to have dinner in on a restaurant?
   B: That would be great, but I am have no money.
   C: Sorry. I'm have broke, too.

Future plans: *be going to* → 4D

Everything's gonna be alright

➕ ➖	I	'm / 'm not	going to	travel tonight. get married soon.
	You	're / aren't		
	He	's / isn't		
❓	Am I / Are you / Is he		going to	be out on Saturday? retire next year?
✅	Yes, I am. / we are. / he is.			
❌	No, I'm not. / we aren't. / he isn't			

6 Circle the correct rule.

Rules
1 Use the verb **be** *before / after* **going to**.
2 Use the *–ing form /an infinitive verb* after **going to**.
3 Use **going to** + verb to talk about *every day / a plan*.
4 In short answers, *repeat / don't repeat* **going to**.
5 '*I'm gonna work*' means '*I'm going to work*' / '*I worked*'.

7 Put the missing word in each sentence.

1 John ˢ going to study this afternoon.
2 Olga isn't going take a taxi home.
3 Jorge not going to get a new job.
4 **A:** you going to go to the party? / **B:** Yes, I.

Talking about transport → 4E

How	do	you	get go come	to	work? Sydney?	I	go / come	by car / taxi / bus / train.
				home? from your house?		You	take	a bus / a taxi / the underground.
							(can) drive / cycle / walk = go **on** foot.	

How long does it take (you)?   (It takes) **about half an hour.**
How far is it (from your house)?   (It's about) **about a kilometre.**

8 Study the table. Write T (true) or F (false).

1 It's correct to say *I get by underground*. ___
2 *I go by bus* is the same as *I take a bus*. ___
3 It's correct to say *I take a train*. ___
4 It's correct to say *I go by foot*. ___
5 You can also use the imperative: *Take a taxi. / Get the number 10 bus*. ___
6 In *How long does **it** take?* 'it' refers to 'the journey'. ___

9 Complete the questions and answers.

1 **A:** How do I get _to_ your house ____ the airport?
   B: Take the underground ____ the city centre. Then you can go ____ foot or get ____ taxi.
2 **A:** I often go ____ work ____ train.
   B: How long does ____ usually take?
   A: About ____ hour.
   B: How ____ is it?
   A: ____ exactly 62 kilometres.

Prepositions at the end of questions → 4F

Who			to?
What	are you	talking	about?
Who		chatting	with?

10 Complete the sentences with a preposition.

around   for   on   to   with

1 Last year in China, how did you get *around*?
2 Who did you go _____?
3 How long did you stay there _____?
4 Which floor do you live _____?
5 Where are you driving _____?

Richmond Publishing
4th Floor
26–28 Hammersmith Grove
London
W6 7BA

© Richmond Publishing, 2009

ISBN: 978-84-668-0601-5

Printed by Orymu, S.A.
D.L: M-21893-2011

Project Development: Sarah Thorpe
Editors: Lynda Parkinson, Virginia García
Design and Layout: Nigel Jordan, Phil Wilkes, Lorna Heaslip
Cover Design: Aqueduct, London and Richmond Publishing
Photo Research: Magdalena Mayo
Audio Production: Paul Ruben Productions, Inc. NYC

Richmond Essential English Course is an adaptation of *Interlink* (© Learning Factory, Ltda.)
Published under licence by Learning Factory Ltda.

The publishers would like to thank the original *Interlink* writing team:
Daniela Bertolucci, Carla Chaves, Angela Dias, Sebastião Ferreira, Lilian Lopes, Nelson Mitrano, Ricardo Sili, Rosane Thiebaut

Many thanks to all the wonderful editorial and publishing team at Richmond for their collective creative efforts and hard work throughout, and to Carmen, Lula and Calum for putting up with so many hours of the back of my head – yet again. *(Paul Seligson)*

Every effort has been made to trace the holders of copyright before publication. The publishers will be pleased to rectify any error or omission at the earliest opportunity.

Illustrations:
David Banks, John Bradley, Matt Johnstone, Matt Latchford, Gillian Martin, Ben Swift, Damien Weighill

Photographs:

*F. Ontañón; GARCÍA-PELAYO/Juancho/*CENTRO COMERCIAL SUPERDIPLO; *J. Jaime; J. Lucas; Prats i Camps; S. Enríquez;* A. G. E. FOTOSTOCK/Raymond Forbes, Foodfolio, Peter Phipp/Travels, Frank and Helena Herh; ACI AGENCIA DE FOTOGRAFÍA/Alamy Images; ARIAS FORMATO PROFESIONAL/A. ARIAS; CORDON PRESS/ CORBIS/Bettmann, REUTERS, Christophe Boisvieux, Hemis/Hervé Hughes, JAI/Alan Copson, Peter Mazel, Neal Preston, Zefa/Heinz Mollenhauer, Ramin Talaie, Camera Press; FOTOLIA; FOTONONSTOP/ Mauritius, Tips/ Chuck Pefley; GETTY IMAGES SALES SPAIN/Gallo Images/ Travel Ink, Image Source, Ethan Miller, Jeff Kravitz, AFP/ Jean-Pierre Muller, WireImage/Jon Furniss, Tim Graham, AsiaPix, Photodisc/Ryan McVay, Stone/Siri Stafford, Riser/David Woolley, Stone/Paul Chesley, AFP/ Pierre Boussel, AFP/Henning Kaiser, Taxi/Jim Naughten, Taxi/David Noble, Matthew Stockman, Stone/Tim Brown, Stone/Jon Riley, AFP/Antonio Scorza, Robert Whitaker, Justin Sullivan, Gregor Schuster, George Eastman House/ Victor Keppler, Giuseppe Cacace, Cathlyn Melloan, AFP/Vanderlei Almeida, Medioimages/Photodisc, Premium Archive/Robert Whitaker, Digital Vision/ B2M Productions, Bambu Productions/Taxi, Hulton Archive/Lambert, 3D4Medical.com, Keystone/ Hulton Archive, WireImage/Jordin Althaus, Digital Vision/ Chad Baker, Paul Bradbury, Digital Vision/John Howard, Digital Vision/Allen Simon, Bill Pugliano, The Image Bank/ GSO Images, Photonica/Henrik Sorensen, The Image Bank/ Suzanne Laird, Digital Vision/Javier Pierini, Mike Theiler, Iconica/Jetta Productions, The Image Bank/Cesar Lucas Abreu, Time&Life Pictures/Martha Holmes, Hulton Archive/ Dave Hogan, Time & Life Pictures/Robert Nickelsberg, Ken Straiton; HIGHRES PRESS STOCK/AbleStock.com; ISTOCKPHOTO; PHOTODISC; STOCK PHOTOS/Masterfile, Radius; Yahoo! Inc. FLICKR; CREATIVE LABS; MATTON-BILD; SERIDEC PHOTOIMAGENES CD; ARCHIVO SANTILLANA